Endorsements

Pastor Claude Bevier masterfully takes us into a Word-based world of how a man should be constructed. From our mindset, to reaching our full potential, to the importance of us having proper accountability, this masterpiece leaves no stone unturned when it comes to manhood. With the Word of God and stories from Claude's own assent into his destined place as a man, The Blueprint will serve as a blade sharpener for any man no matter where we are on our journey.

–MONTY WEATHERALL, Pastor and Author of
"Taking My Life Back, Thriving After the Trauma of Childhood Sexual Abuse."

This book will not only Unveil Truths of our God Designed Manhood, but it will Unlock & Unleash a timely touch of our God Designed Mantles! You'll be inspired to pursue even more, not only who you are in Christ, but who Christ is in you! As you read with Hunger, you'll be empowered to receive our *True Identity* as men, fathers, husbands and leaders!

–SAMUEL A. SEGUNDO JR.
Pastor, Conference Speaker, Network Founder, Church Consultant & Financial Expert
President - Family Faith Center, Inc.
Founder - S&C Ministries, Inc.
Co-Founder - Relate Ministerial Network, Inc

If You Want to Experience All That God Has Destined for You, The Blueprint Is Essential. In it, Pastor Claude Bevier Gives Helpful and Relevant Tools That You Can Use to Reach A Place of Influence and Impact. This Book Will Help You Progress from Being A Good Man to Being A GREAT Man!

–BISHOP STEVEN M., Ar̃ ' ' ‾
City of Gra

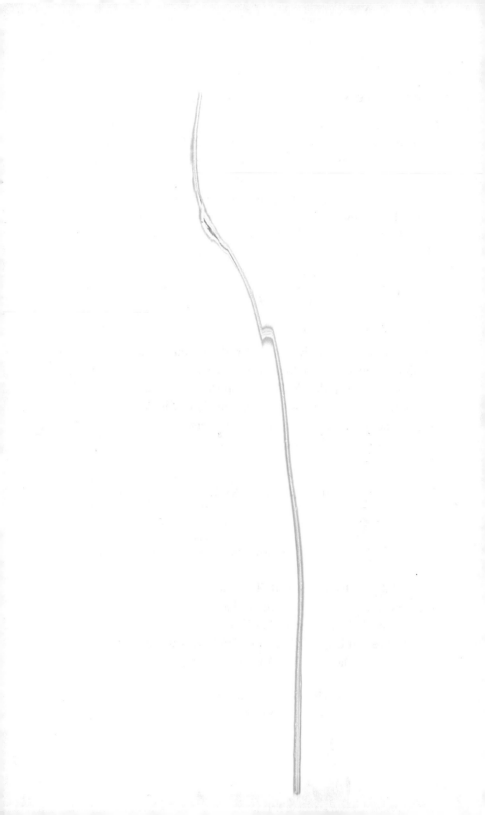

THE
BLUEPRINT

A Man's Journey to Self Discovery

THE
BLUEPRINT

A Man's Journey to Self Discovery

CLAUDE BEVIER

Trilogy Christian Publishing

Trilogy Christian Publishers
A Wholly Owned Subsidiary of Trinity Broadcasting Network

2442 Michelle Drive
Tustin, CA 92780

For information, address Trilogy Christian Publishing

Rights Department, 2442 Michelle Drive, Tustin, CA 92780.

Trilogy Christian Publishing/ TBN and colophon are trademarks of Trinity Broadcasting Network.

For information about special discounts for bulk purchases, please contact Trilogy Christian Publishing.

Manufactured in the United States of America

10 9 8 7 6 5 4 3 2 1

Library of Congress Cataloging-in-Publication Data is available.

ISBN#: 978-1-64088-101-3

ISBN#: 978-1-64088-102-0 (E-book)

Dedication

To my Heavenly Father, The Lord Jesus and the precious Holy Spirit - for Fathering me and revealing to me my purpose. My life is forever indebted to your service.

To my Awesome, Anointed, Faithful, Loving, Supportive Wife Rosa L. Bevier- You have been on this journey with me since we were teenagers. You have dreamed this dream with me. We went from being homeless, to sleeping in a car and eating blue cheese from a glass jar at a fireplace in a vacant home, to Pastoring God's people and influencing the lives of many. Therefore, I celebrate you because you deserve it my Queen. Thank you for allowing me to grow as a Man while being your husband and our children's Father. I truly love you and want the world to know that there is no me without you. This is our accomplishment, this is our victory, this is our dream!

To Dr's William and Veronica Winston - Your living example and words have revolutionized my life. Thank you for always creating and environment for your Sons and Daughters to grow.

To Pastors Henry and Connie Healey - You poured your lives out unto us and I am forever grateful for how you believed in a young Man who had no direction at all in life. You gave me the opportunity to *Become.* I received the *Blueprint* as your youth Pastor.

To the late Dr. Myles Munroe - For your passion and desire to see Men walk in their full potential, some of your last words were fuel to my faith pertaining to writing this book. It is my prayer that I can humbly add to the great foundation you have built, concerning Manhood.

To all the Fathers and Men - Who have overcome great obstacles as I have and have tirelessly and selflessly served your marriages, families, churches, communities and country. I wrote this book for you and I pray that it adds to your faith. I salute you all.

To every Fatherless child - God loves you and hears your cry, He said He will be a Father to the fatherless. Don't give up, you are not alone.

Foreword

Reaching thousands of children in over 21 years, I have had the personal experience of ministering to a fatherless generation. I have seen how a young man that is not fathered, is at a high percentage rate of becoming a statistic in this world because he has no identity. My wife and I founded Church of Joy, Reach A Generation in 1997. I am committed to ministering to the whole family, and to do that it is vital to help men to be the man of God, He created him to be. I encourage men according to Malachi 4:5-6 (NKJV) where God said He would turn the hearts of fathers back to their children. I have authored two books, "Reach A Generation" and "The Spirit and Power of Elijah". This is a strong connection that brought Pastor Claude and myself together. Building men up so they can turn their hearts to their wives and to their children, and to fulfill their destiny.

I had the privilege of meeting Pastor Claude Bevier almost 20 years ago. I invited him to minister to my young people when he was a Christian Rap Artist and minister. His message and music were so well received. Pastor Claude shared candidly his story of tragedy as a young person, a story our young people could relate to. Pastor Claude brought this young generation at my ministry hope. They got a revelation at a young age that if God could change Pastor Claude's life then he could change their life. It was through men like Pastor Claude that helped spark hope in my young people as I would share with them weekly that God has a purpose for their lives, and through that I saw thousands of young people give their life to Jesus.

Today, I am so proud to see Pastor Claude, the founder and Senior Pastor of Restore World Church, pastoring a beautiful and thriving church, and ministering a powerful message God has given him for men. His life story would make any man's heart hard, yet he allowed God to soften his heart to bring the love of God to his family, to his church and a bold message for men. Pastor

Claude's revelation "But I know Him, for I am from Him, and He sent Me." John 7:29 (NKJV) as he has said, was his roadmap to manhood. Finding intimacy with God, finding his identity from God, and finding his Destiny through God. This book will bring you to a place of knowing you exist for God's purpose and plan, and through this revelation Pastor Claude received from God, He has given you the blueprint for who you are and what you are destined to do. *"Change the men and Change the world"* Pastor Claude Bevier

I am grateful God caused our paths to cross, we have the same heart for a young generation, for men, and for the family. With what our Nation is facing today, and the crisis that the family is facing daily, Pastor Claude and I are standing for men and their families. This book has answers that will not only change men but will leave a blueprint for generations to come. We are standing, praying and encouraging men across the Nation to turn their hearts to God and to their families which begins with THE BLUEPRINT.

−PASTOR LUIS R. REYES
Founder / Senior Pastor
Church of Joy, Reach A Generation − Waukegan, Illinois

Preface

I have been saying for years, *If we just change one thing, we can change the whole world.* I see it in my mind clearly, yet it's sometimes difficult to explain. Imagine building a beautiful home but failing to lay the proper foundation. It wouldn't matter how beautiful the walls, the ceiling, the floors were; it wouldn't matter what kind of furniture and window treatment we put in the house, eventually there would be a major problem. The house would begin to shift and become unstable because there was no proper foundation to build it on. This is what society is facing today. We have been trying to address the trauma families are experiencing today without going to the root of the issue or recognizing that it's impossible to build family properly without getting the Male Man in his proper place. It is absolutely evident that when the Male Man is out of his place, the entire family suffers.

What's even more evident is that today, more than ever, we are seeing a generation of Males who have no true understanding or concept of what it is to be a Man. This is a product and consequence of Males growing up without Fathers. Due to the lack of proper Fathering, the image of the Male Man is being diminished and looked down on in society. Men have grown tired, men have grown weary. The pressure Men are facing today is nothing less than overwhelming. Over the years I have been able to see the tragic shift that has happened where men have lost their sense of value, thus losing confidence in who they are and resulting in ineffectiveness when it comes to leading their family. It's almost as if the enemy has strategically focused on the Male Man as his target, knowing that if he can cause the Man to fall, he can cause society to fall. I have been completely consumed with the idea of recognizing and addressing this whole Manhood issue, and I am also aware that it's impossible to fix the Manhood issue without first addressing the number one Epidemic of Fatherlessness. The Fatherhood-Manhood connection is what I believe, when addressed, will change society for the better. Ignoring this has resulted in the divorce rate at an all-time high both inside and outside of the church. Children have been affected tremendously by this and are being raised without the love and affirmation of their natural father in the home. Young men especially, have grown cold and indifferent, angry and violent.

Just recently I woke up, and as I generally do every day had my routine of prayer, study, and then eventually coffee with my wife. After that, I usually check my schedule, emails and then I move to all of our personal and business bank accounts. That's pretty much my mornings on a daily basis. This particular day I got on social media and I was stunned; another school shooting. I began to see the news, the pictures of families crying, students crying, and my heart just sunk. I couldn't believe it. I recall looking at the picture of the young man who killed all those innocent people and thought to myself, "How can an individual be so cold hearted;" I then reflected on previous school shootings and even some of the other similar acts of violence involving our youth and discovered they all had one thing in common, *Fatherlessness.* Unfortunately, I saw exactly what I knew I would see: another fatherless child. Often, we hear people say, "if we had better politicians things would be better, if we had better policies and procedures things would be better, if we had better jobs, better schools, better trade skills programs, better, better, better!" The list could go on for days. It seems we keep dealing with the fruit of the matter and never going to the root of the matter. We keep trying to build beautiful homes without laying the proper foundation. Now more than ever, we must address the real issues at hand, and that is helping Men to see themselves as God sees them. Helping them to realize their true God given potential, helping them to discover their identity through a close intimate personal relationship with God as Father through Jesus Christ.

In this book we will do just that, we will deal with The Fatherhood-

Manhood connection, and how it has impacted a Man's perception of himself. We are going to construct you from the inside out and help every Man to become the best man he can be. I still believe in real Manhood, the kind of Men that sacrificially lives in order to better his family and his community. I still believe in the concept of family from a biblical perspective where the Male Man is the foundation of his household. I still believe "If we can change one thing, we can change the whole world."

The Blueprint

Acknowledgements

This book has taken me almost 20 years to complete. Not that I've been writing for twenty years, but I've been growing and developing for all those years. I remember in my younger years being hungry to succeed and accomplish great things. I also remember crying out to God saying, "Why is it taking so long." I even got a prophecy that "My Footprint of Fatherhood would cover the Globe," but it seemed like it was never going to happen. I am so glad it didn't happen in those years; I wasn't ready then. This process called *The Blueprint* is now a proven system that has worked in the development of the lives of many men; both young and older alike. It has been the collective contribution also of many individuals that has made this dream and vision come to pass. I recognize that without all of these people, this book would not have come to pass, so I would like to acknowledge all of you.

I want to thank my beautiful wife Rosa for always supporting me and believing in me. Thank you to my two beautiful daughters Nicole and Victoria; also my two remarkable Sons in love, Darren and Michael; my three beautiful G Babies, Jordan, Favor and Flourish. Thank you all for participating in this whole process. Thank you for sharing me with the world and all of your peers that call me "Dad." Thank you to Gerod and Stephani Sturgis and your beautiful family. Thanks G, for seeing the greatness in me and owning the vision just like it was your own. Thanks Steph for all that you do, especially helping me construct this life-changing book. Thank you Rangariro Mutatu and Phillip Hammond for your creative direction in this book, thanks to my mother Sharon Pickett, my brother Charles, my sisters Andrea and Brenda, my brother in Love Tim, and all my family, I love all of you. We have endured many obstacles and have overcome them all. Thank you to my Restore World Church family, both in Adrian, and Romulus, Michigan. Thank you to my awesome staff and thank you to all of my "Children," you all know who you are. It would take too much space to name all of you! Thank you for allowing me to be your father and give you what Jesus has given me, "Dad" Loves you. Thanks to my Pastors Dr. Bill and Veronica Winston, your words have changed my life, I would not be here without you. Thank you, Pastors Henry and Connie Healey, for pouring into our lives, we are forever thankful for your years of wisdom, Thanks to Pastor Sam and Christina Segundo, Bishop Steven and Regina Arnold, Pastors Stephan and Micheline Lorenz, Pastors Tommy and Brandi Stevenson, Pastor Larry Mack, Minister Marketa Mack, Pastors Monte and Kimberly Weatherall, Pastors Louis and Trisha Reyes, Ministers Derrick and Miriam Collins and all of my FMA family. Finally, thank you to TBN, Trilogy Publishing, Matt Crouch, Rhett Harwell, Bryan Norris, Kim Hook, Misty, and all who played a part in making this book a success.

Introduction

Oftentimes as a Male Man we are faced with so many struggles and obstacles in life. These things can seem so insurmountable in scope or view due to our lack of knowledge pertaining to who we are as Men. There is this idea that Manhood is equated to how much success you have or how much money you have or how firm of a handshake you have, and even though these are all great qualities, they have nothing to do with what it is to be a Man!

Growing up without my natural Father in my life due to his tragic death when I was 4 years old, and having a great Step Father but still having no true leadership due to his own lack of knowledge in the area of Manhood, left me with emptiness and a void concerning what it was to be a Man. This emptiness and void became the fuel in my life that drove me to invest countless hours of studying, praying, and discovering what it was to understand my Maleness.

It was shortly after my Step Father's death at my young age of 28 that I began my journey of self-discovery. I was born again at the age of 20 and married my girlfriend (Rosa) at that time and began to raise a family without having any real understanding of what it meant to be a Man, let alone a husband or Father. My frustration as a Male was indescribable! I could only say that though I had been saved and married and everything was supposed to be good, I felt like an absolute failure! I had this awesome responsibility of being the head of a family and had no idea what I was doing. I was a mess, an accident not waiting to happen but an accident happening Daily!

The only real example of what it was to be a Man was what I discovered in the local church. This environment became the place where I would plant myself, and my family and I would then do what I call "On the Job Training". I began to glean from other men in the local church and emulate them, their habits and behavior; I even started dressing like them and talking like them. They were my only source to try and discover myself, and although it helped me it was still shallow, I still felt like something was missing in my life as a Male Man. I was terrified but something on the inside of me knew there was more to this Man thing, and though I couldn't put my finger on it I knew it existed, and if it existed I had to discover it.

In my desperation I began to delve and to dig into God's word and I fell upon one simple small verse of scripture that revolutionized my life! Jesus said in John 7:29 *"For I know him, I am from him; he hath sent me"*. This verse of scripture seemed to leap off the page and it was as if this verse belonged only to me! Now for the first time in my life I could see clearly, I could become what I knew existed beyond what I was seeing, I could become a Man! This verse became my roadmap to manhood. It would soon become the single most important truth that I would learn and build my life from.

Here is how I saw it that day, "I KNOW him (Intimacy), I AM from him (Identity); he hath SENT me (Destiny). This revelation of this simple small verse of scripture became what I NOW call *The Blueprint*. A Blueprint is something you use as a reference or a guide when building something like an office complex or a house and many other things. It's the plans that were designed beforehand in order that the builder might build accordingly.

Growing up, I remember I would always get a bike, game, or some gift that required assembly. The plans for assembly were included with the purchase, but due to my excessive desire to ride the bike or play with the game I just looked at the picture on the outside of the box and didn't use the plans to assemble it correctly. When I was done it looked right but didn't function correctly.

This is how it's been with us as Men; we have the desire to be great and accomplish great things, and in our desperation to achieve, we look at the lives of other men and began to assemble our lives by what we see in their lives, and we come up short because many of our examples of Manhood lacked knowledge themselves. So many men have been hurt and wounded, and have internalized these hurts and wounds, and out of them have developed mindsets that were wrong and passed them down to their sons and daughters. This cycle of ignorance pertaining to our Maleness is why we have not been functioning correctly, we have been malfunctioning. Hosea 4:6 states that "due to the lack of knowledge (in any given area) we perish." To perish is to fail or to be destroyed, and that's what's happening to men from every walk of life! Due to the lack of Biblical knowledge of how to build and develop our lives as Men we have been (failing) and have become comfortable with functioning in dysfunction!

Some would probably say "Claude, that's not fair, you're making an accusation against my Manhood." My answer is No! I'm simply making an observation based upon what is evident in society. Families are being destroyed, children are hurting. We are experiencing the highest rates of suicide, teenage pregnancy, incarceration, substance abuse, multiple school shootings and much more. We are seeing things in this generation we never thought we would see ever and it's because of this dysfunctional Image of Manhood. Now we have built dysfunctional marriages and have raised dysfunctional families and out of that grew dysfunctional Churches, communities, neighborhoods, cities, states, countries and resulting in a dysfunction world. One of today's most effective leaders, John Maxwell, states "Everything rises or falls based upon leadership" and leadership starts with the Male Man!

This book you are holding in your hand right now is, in my opinion, the answer to the many problems we face today as men. It addresses the many questions we have asked as men. Yes, this is a

"Man's Book" and I aim to take you on a journey of self-discovery that will empower you to come into being everything you have been originally intended to be as a Man. Make this reading your priority and dive into it with great expectation, and I believe you will come out on the other side a NEW MAN.

This book is also for women; if you are a wife and you are reading this, keep reading, because this book will empower you to know some of the struggles and challenges we as Men face daily. It will inform you by helping you to understand why so many men are unhappy and unfulfilled. After reading this book you will be able to be the *Help Meet* God has designed you to be, and help your Man of God fulfill his potential. If you are a single woman don't put it down, learn the qualities of a Man so when you are ready to date one of these awesome Men you will have foreknowledge that will equip you to make proper choices pertaining to who you date and potentially marry. Lastly, if you are a parent then you need to get this in your children's library, because every young Male Man needs this book for his personal development, and every daughter needs this book so she will be equipped with proper information and will know what to look for within a Male.

I'm excited, this book has been in the making for almost 20 years and you and I together are about to "Change the men and Change this World".

> – CLAUDE BEVIER, Founder and Pastor of
> Restore World Church Adrian and Romulus
> Michigan. Also the founder of Restore World Tour.

Table of Contents

SECTION 1
INTIMACY

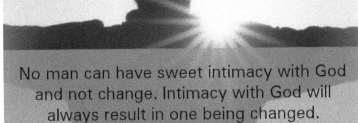

No man can have sweet intimacy with God and not change. Intimacy with God will always result in one being changed.

CHAPTER 1

UNVEILING THE SYSTEM

PSALM 37:4

*"Delight yourself also in the LORD,
and He shall give you the desires of your heart."*

Breaking the Intimacy Barrier

We live in a society where the focus is emphasized on productivity, achievement, goal setting, and success. By nature, as men we are hunters so we like the sense of conquering something. We like the fact that we signed the contract, got the raise, sealed the deal, won the game, accomplished the dream, and actualized our ideas. When men gather together into a room we don't like to talk about intimate things, we don't like to necessarily share our weaknesses or engage in dialogue that's vulnerable because we deem those type of conversations feminine or weak, after all we are Men and as a Man we aren't supposed to exhibit weakness or express anything in an effeminate manner. This type of mindset has clouded our perception and left many of us as men empty, and without real concrete answers to the questions we have pertaining to our Maleness. It then is imperative that we discover from a biblical perspective what real Manhood is and renew our thinking that our paradigm can be changed so that we can realize our full potential as Men.

During the course of this book I will make reference to a Men's Ministry I have developed called "The Turn Challenge." This Ministry is, in my opinion, one of the greatest Men's programs ever developed because it literally reconstructs a man by reconstructing his concept of what Manhood really is. We start first of all, before anything else with the subject of "Intimacy" and God's idea of it in a Man's life. Almost every time when discussing the subject of "Intimacy" I find it to be the hardest thing to discuss with men, because men have a tendency to want to skip past it and move to something more logical or more palatable and acceptable to how they have been raised. What I have also discovered is if we don't master the "Intimacy Level", then the other levels never really work.

In the book of Psalms, chapter 37:4, the writer says, "Delight yourself also in the lord, and he shall give you the desires of your heart." When it comes to the subject of "Intimacy" when dealing with manhood, this verse has become one of the most important verses in the bible for me! It's often read like this "Seek God and he will give you what you want", but that's not what it says at all. Often, we read the scripture with a mindset that it's all about us, and this selfish, narcissistic way of thinking has left so many Men broken and unfulfilled because we've made it all about us.

When I began to look at this in depth, I discovered that the word "Delight" is a powerful word that means to be "Soft or Pliable" or effeminate. When we are pliable it means we are susceptible to being led or directed, capable of being shaped or bent or drawn out. It also paints a picture of an individual that can readily adjust and adapt to God's will and plan for his life. This verse is saying the person that has surrendered through Intimacy with God and his word is able to be led, molded, shaped into what God has desired for that individual; God's desires become his desires and they are able to become and fulfill everything God has predestined them to do.

As a pastor of a local Church I get the opportunity to see men often. I get to watch them weekly, and even sometimes more than that concerning their relationships with their wives and children. I also get to see how they treat others. I have discovered that a Man who loves and surrenders to God will always love and surrender to his family. Jesus deals with this in Matthew's gospel when being questioned about the great commandment. Jesus says (Matthew 22:37-40) "That we should love God, love ourselves and then love others." This is what I call love capacity. It shows that when a man has a problem loving and honoring his wife, children and others, it's directly connected to his personal, Intimate relationship with God as Father. This is exactly what the Apostle Paul was saying in Ephesians 5:28, "So ought men to love their wives as their own bodies. He that loveth his wife loveth himself." The evidence that a Man loves himself is in how he expresses Love to his wife and others, and it's clear in Matthew's gospel that for a Man to love himself he must first Love God! This is the Level of Intimacy....

I often get up in front of my congregation and see women raising their hands and tears running down their faces as they fully surrender to God in worship. It's rare that you see men raising their hands, crying out to God in total dependency upon him. I believe this has everything to do with our view of intimacy with God and how it relates to our perception of Manhood. Most men cannot equate real Manhood with Intimacy, and because of this it has caused us to be guarded in this area.

Being a Pastor also gives me opportunity to counsel multiple marriages, and the one common area that pops up from women concerning their marriages is that they say the man doesn't express his emotions. What they really are saying is "My husband lacks real intimacy." Now concerning marriage and intimacy, most of us men equate intimacy with sex! This is unfortunate because sexual intimacy is the lowest form of intimacy in the marriage, although a definite benefit in the marriage. Any man who has been married any significant amount of time knows that when a woman is speaking of intimacy she is speaking of communication, vulnerability and opening himself up in certain areas. Unfortunately, this breakdown in understanding intimacy from a Man's view versus a woman's view has caused tons of marriages to end tragically in divorce. I read an article on Marriage and Divorce from the American Psychological Association that said 90 percent of people marry by the age of 50, but 40 to 50 percent of marriages in the United States end in divorce and the divorce rate for subsequent marriages is even higher. It's very obvious there's a problem. I often tell couples during marriage counseling love is not that mushy, gushy, wushy feeling you have for the individual right now; love is that lifetime commitment you have when you begin to see that he or she doesn't necessarily see things your way or perhaps they don't clean the house your way or wash the clothes your way! These statistics are staggering, and I believe they are the result of individuals not knowing who they are, and this lack of personal value surfaces in the lives of men and women alike, and consequently many end up divorced because of this. I have discovered that a Man's intimate relationship with God empowers him to have the stability necessary to stick it out in his marriage, family, or any responsibility he has, regardless of the challenges he may be facing.

I think it's time we as men change our perception when it comes to the area of intimacy. Let's look at this in the life of Jesus. My favorite scripture in the whole bible is found in the book of Hebrew 5:7, and it says, "Who in the days of his flesh, he (Jesus) offered up prayers, supplication, strong crying and tears unto him who was able to save him from death and he was heard because he feared God." Wow! Every time I meditate that verse it paints a picture of Jesus completely dependent upon the Father through intimacy with him.

This was the lifestyle Jesus lived, and this is why he was so effective during his life here on earth. Jesus was constantly finding places where he could separate himself and continue to develop his intimate relationship with his heavenly father (Read Mark 1:35, Luke 6:12). Jesus was always governed and directed as a man by the Holy Spirit (Read Luke 4:4 AMP). Jesus never did his own will or desires; his will was to accomplish what the Father sent him here to do (Read John 5:19 and John 6:38). Jesus, in my opinion, is the best example to emulate as a Man who absolutely, unequivocally delighted himself in the lord. Therefore, as men we must look to HIM for what it means to BE a Man and redefine our view of intimacy. Often times we look to Jesus as savior, and yes this is very necessary, yet at the same time we must look to him as our example for living. I like how one Man of God says, "Jesus is The sample son." Even in the book of Hebrew chapter 12:2, scripture teaches we should look to Jesus who is the author and finisher of our faith, and I believe as we look to him we are empowered as Men to emulate his example.

Discovering the Pattern

John 7:29 "For I know him, I am from him; he hath sent me."

It was the year 1998, and I was pacing back and forth praying in an upstairs classroom in the local church I attended and served in for almost 6 years by then. I was a traveling gospel rapper and was experiencing some success but hadn't yet become known to the point that I could travel full time. The reason I was pacing was because just a week or so before this moment, my pastor asked me to "Go in that teen ministry and take it over". As I continued to pace and pray, I was reflecting on my life and questioning God about it. My plea was a desperate plea because I had a very challenging upbringing. I never completed high school but eventually accomplished getting a high school equivalent (GED). All of my teenage years were squandered by my bad choices, and as far as me going to any college and getting an education at that time didn't seem logical, because I needed to be responsible and work to provide for my young wife and two very young daughters. On top of that, the teen ministry wasn't doing great at all. There were about 5 youth in it and 6 or 7 parents that were desperately coming, trying to figure out how to keep their children in church. I guess I was the last hope at that time. My prayer was a cry to God; What am I supposed to do with my life God? After crying out to him, I began to search his word and found the verse that changed my life; John 7:29. This was Jesus talking, It was written in red, it leaped off the page to me and became the foundation of everything I do in my life now almost 20 years later. I saw it as three principles for living: know God, know yourself, and know your purpose in life. Later it became what I now call *The Blueprint: Intimacy, Identity and Destiny.* God always helps me retain the things he teaches me in rhyming words or acronyms. That day when I discovered that verse it empowered me with faith, I knew then that no matter what my past has been, no matter what my record was, no matter what my education was, if I would just follow this pattern for living then I would be a successful MAN!

Once I found this truth, I then began to search the bible for patterns because I believe God has patterns that he operates by. Patterns imply consistent behavior and I needed to know this was a consistent behavior for God. What I discovered was almost overwhelming, because I discovered this was not only a consistent pattern for him, but it was literally his only pattern for developing Men! I then discovered that not only was it the exclusive way, but it was his original way. Wow! I fell upon a gold mine when it comes
to how God functions.

"Restore" It's Time to Go Back!

Years ago, I learned that if you want to know the end of a thing then you needed to go back to the beginning of it and research its original intention. Jesus was not just the savior that would free mankind from their sin, but he was also the "Redeemer" that would buy back humanity with his personal sacrifice and restore mankind back to what God originally intended for all of us. The word *Restore* is a fascinating word in the Hebrew Language. It's the Hebrew word "Shuv" and it means *to go back to the original or movement back to the point of departure.* It implies that through the fall of man we left God's original intention for our lives as men and got off track and are in need of regaining what was lost! Here is another analogy for this word *Restore.* If you and I were to buy an old 1975 Trans Am which happens to be the first car I ever owned, and we decided to *Restore* it, we would have to find out what it looked like, what kind and size engine was in it, what it was equipped with, even down to color and tires. After doing the research, in order to *Restore* it we would have to make it exactly the same as the original. What does this have to do with manhood? I'm glad you asked. Just like we would have to do research on everything that was original pertaining to my 1975 Trans Am, we have to research the scripture and discover God's original design and intention for man and allow that to be the pattern we emulate and strive to be like.

"Repent" Change Your Thinking as a Man

I previously said this *Blueprint* I discovered was God's pattern for developing Men. Again the *Blueprint* is found in John 7:29 and it is threefold: Intimacy, Identity and Destiny. Knowing God enables you and I to know ourselves and knowing ourselves enables us to know what God put us here for. During the course of this book I will point this pattern out in the lives of many Men of God to help you see clearly that this is a proven system that works for Men to come into being everything God has created us to be. I'm going to start with this *Blueprint* in the life of Adam but, in order for me to do that I must first start with Jesus and his message he taught which was *"The Gospel of The Kingdom of God."* When teaching this message, he used a very interesting phrase "Repent ye and believe the Gospel." We are going to look at this statement in depth.

When Jesus came his message was not only a message of deliverance from sin, slavery and bondage, but his message was a message of restoration, reinstatement, and recovery of what Men lost through the fall of man. Let's see this in the book of Mark. In the inception of Jesus' Ministry, it says in Mark 1:14-15 *"Now after that John was put in prison, Jesus came into Galilee, PREACHING the Gospel of the KINGDOM of GOD, 15. And saying, "The time is fulfilled, and the Kingdom of God is at hand: REPENT YE, and BELIEVE the Gospel.*

This scripture has 4 key elements we must review in our research of God's original plan concerning Manhood.

1. Jesus began preaching the Gospel (Gospel here means Good News)

2. The Good news was: The Kingdom was at hand (The word Kingdom means God's rule, reign, royalty, realm, and reality in Man is at our grasp) this means we must seize it!

3. It was fulfilled then, not in the future!

4. Repent (Means to Change our Thinking.)

5. Let's discover exactly what Jesus meant when he said "Repent Ye and Believe." The word repent is a Greek word Metanoeo and it means to think differently or afterwards, to reconsider.

Also, the word *Repent* is made up of two greek words: *Meta* denoting change of place or condition, and *Noeo* that denotes perceiving with the mind or to think or comprehend. Therefore, when Jesus was teaching here he literally was saying, "I am here, it's fulfilled, you don't have to live in sin any longer, you don't have to miss what God originally intended you to be or do, quit thinking like a slave, THINK LIKE THE MAN YOU ARE, YOU'RE MADE IN GOD'S IMAGE! Change your thinking and that will enable you to change your Lives!

Another way to look at this word *Repent* is to understand that it's a compound word; two words put together to make one word and give us understanding. The first word is RE- which means to go back or do again. This word is used in words like remark, reevaluate, reschedule, resource, replenish, it speaks of going back, redoing something. The second word is PENT: like it's used concerning penthouse, you always see a penthouse "at the TOP." Again, Jesus was trying again to tell us "Go BACK to Thinking like God created you to think, you've been created to think like your heavenly Father. Think like you are on TOP, and your Life— circumstances, situations, families, marriages, health— will then change. This is a powerful understanding here that will help us as Men draw our conclusion of what real Manhood is, from the very first Man God created. Now we will take a look at the link between the first Man Adam and the last Adam; Jesus.

Jesus is Identi ied with Adam

1ˢᵗ Corinthians 15:45 and so it is written, the first man Adam was made a living soul; the last Adam was made a quickening spirit.

The Apostle Paul makes a connection between Adam and The Lord Jesus by calling Jesus "The Last Adam", identifying Jesus with Adam. This is so important when understanding Manhood. As I mentioned earlier, our problem as Men has been our lack of proper male figures that we are to emulate. Just recently, I was being interviewed in Detroit, Michigan, by an awesome Father figure in the city. This Man of God is making a tremendous impact in the city of Detroit. During the interview he and I were discussing this whole Manhood issue. The pastor asked me a question about the hurt and failure we see in the lives of most young men today. He said to me "What do you think these young men are crying out for?" My answer was simple, I told him they are crying out for a Father, they are looking for someone to look up to, someone to give them identity and tell them who they are. Not only do young Men need Natural Male figures to look up to, they also need to SEE Jesus as an attainable source of what it is to be Male. Here's what I mean. Often we are taught that the life of Jesus is so unattainable. This incorrect teaching focuses on the divinity of Jesus without properly reflecting on his humanity. That's what I love about this verse! It makes a clear connection that Jesus was a picture of what God intended Adam to be. It's as if the apostle Paul, by inspiration of the Holy Spirit, is saying "Men, if you want to see how you are to live in this life then let Jesus be your example." To better understand, I'll make it clear Jesus is the full picture of what you and I are supposed to be like as Men. Well someone is probably saying "Pastor Claude, That's Ludicrous! Well my response to whoever says that is this: The bible gives you and I full permission and right to emulate every aspect of who Jesus was when he walked the earth. Ephesians 5:1-2 tells us to imitate him, follow his example. When it comes to LOVE everyone says, "let's be like Jesus", but the truth is that every Man has the right to emulate him in every area.

I like what my pastor always says, and I think it's worth repeating, Jesus didn't come to show off, he came to show us. Glory to God, that right there should put some hot sauce on your Chicken. I'm telling you Men of God, we must go back to thinking like Men, Men made in the Image and in the likeness of God and we will see our marriages healed, our children saved and fulfilling their potential. We will see our businesses grow and become successful and our churches, communities, and everything else will perfectly fall in line when we see ourselves as Men that are just like Jesus!

Another scripture that invites you and me as Men to be like Jesus is found in Romans 8:29, and it says, "For whom he did foreknow,   **32** he also did predestinate to be conformed to the Image of his Son (Jesus) that he might be the Firstborn among many brethren." Look at that Man of God. God planned in his foreknowledge that you and I be exactly like Jesus as Men. I like the part that says "Firstborn", that means there's a second, third, fourth, fiftieth, thousandth, and so on. You and I have been given right to be Just like Jesus and remember Jesus while on the earth didn't come as God! He came as a Man dependent upon God the Holy Spirit. He did absolutely nothing as God but everything as a MAN! That means what he did was exactly what God intended to do through Adam before he fell and what he intends to do through YOU right now! Glory to God, now just receive that in Jesus Name. Amen.

Before the Fall

Somehow, when reflecting on the life of Adam the first man, we tend to always default back to his life after the fall of man. It's difficult for most people when reading the bible to see him based upon what God as Father originally intended for him. As I mentioned earlier on I discovered *The Blueprint: Intimacy, Identity and Destiny* was God's system of developing men, and I wanted to point this out in the lives of many starting with Adam.

When I first saw *The Blueprint* in the life of Jesus in John 7:29, God gave me a desire and a special Grace to research his word to see it throughout the bible. I learned if you wanted to know the end of a thing then you had to go back and see it from the beginning. I challenged myself to take what I had discovered as a New Testament truth concerning this *Blueprint* and solidify it by proving it was God's original pattern from the beginning. For me to do this I first needed to ask the Holy Spirit to show it to me, and when I petitioned him about this, he did exactly that! I began to search the scripture and see this "Blueprint" everywhere I looked. It was amazing.

The Blueprint in the Life of Adam

When reading the first few chapters of the bible, if you're not cautious you can almost get to the place where you think "Yeah, I've read that creation stuff, and yeah I know God made man in his image, and yeah I know he gave him dominion and all that, and yeah, I also know man fell into sin through disobedience and high treason and lost it all." We can actually get comfortable with the text and miss out on revelation the Holy Spirit has for us. So, when approaching God's word, we must carefully muse and meditate the word, and in doing this we will see some fascinating things. The psalmist wrote in 119:18 "Open thou my eyes that I may behold wondrous things out of thy law." This kind of attitude towards God's word has to be the driving force of our desire to know the things of God. Daily we have to pray this way and come with an open heart and a fresh desire to know him, and God will answer our cry, he will give us our desire to know him more.

As I began to study I noticed in Genesis 1:26-30 we see God as father communicating with the man. I literally picture the Father with his son, giving specific instruction to him. I am a songwriter, so I love to write songs that make people SEE what I'm SAYING. When I read that the Father released The Blessing upon his son's life in verse 28, and in verse 29, I see God as Father intimately instructing Adam pertaining to dietary laws, animal life, plant life, and how it relates to his position as ruler in the earth, I SEE it happening in my mind. I SEE Adam walking with his Father as his Father instructs him concerning how he has herbs and seed he can plant in order to get the harvest of vegetation that he might eat. I personally believe religion has crippled our imagination of him as father by always referring to our father as "GOD."

A Clear Picture of Intimacy and Identity

I once again SAW this intimate relationship of son and father in chapter 2:7 where Moses paints this vivid picture of what happened in Genesis chapter 1:26. God intimately forms the man from the dust of the ground and breathes into his nostrils the breath of life and man "Came into being a living soul". This verse brings the *Blueprint* out very clearly. When I looked up the word "breath" in Hebrew I found one of the meanings was "Divine Inspiration." This really helped me SEE here, because this verse paints an intimate picture of God as Father giving his son Adam (Identity). Well Pastor Claude, where do you get that from? I thought this verse always meant that God blew in his nose and inflated the man like a balloon. No, that's not what happened at all. When you look at the word breath again it speaks of "Divine Inspiration", and in 1st Timothy 3:16 KJV says "All scripture is given by INSPIRATION of God" but when you look at the amplified version of that same verse it says, "All scripture is God Breathed (Given by Divine Inspiration)". Can you see it now? What really happened is that God released himself through words into the man and the man "Came into being" a living soul. Now we can't stop here with this because as a man thinketh, so is he. You and I are a direct reflection of how we see ourselves, and we must have a point of reference to emulate in order that we can strive for this Manhood from a biblical perspective. This same verse was translated in the Onkelos Aramaic translation from the original Hebrew like this, "God breathed into the Man's nostrils the breath of life and the man became another speaking spirit like God." Glory! Let's not stop there either, because we are looking to SEE not just intimacy but also identity in this verse.

God's Very Own DNA

I remember reading some material from a well-known Greek scholar who is very trusted in our particular community of faith. He began to discuss the subject of fingerprints and things like DNA. When reading his material, a spark was lit within me when he moved even further to talk about what is called "Breath prints." This subject had me absolutely intrigued because whenever anyone talks on the subject of identity, I am all ears. I began to dig to see if what he was saying was true, and lo and behold there it was, a scientific research done on the subject of "Breath prints." The article said that scientist recruited volunteers to blow into a mass spectrometer, a machine often used in chemistry to separate chemical components of different samples. Within seconds, the mass spectrometer spits out results for each person. What they discovered is that a unique core signature always underlies a person's breath. This means we are identifiable by our breath. They literally said that in the future "Breath prints" could become the new urine test. Well what does this mean? Our DNA is traceable in our breath! Glory to God! This means when God breathed into Adam, he was releasing his very own DNA within his son!!!! This brings a whole new understanding to what it means to be made in his Image and Likeness. When the writer is speaking of God breathing here, he is speaking of God releasing words (His very own self) within the man. This means God's DNA is within his word, and when we as Men get intimately acquainted with him through reading and meditating his word, God literally is Fathering us, giving us Identity. If we as men would just meditate on this occurrence here in scripture, it would eliminate every trace of fear, low self-esteem, inadequacy, inferiority, and all insignificance in a man's life.

If you will notice that after Jesus was raised from the dead, during his great commission in John 20:21 Jesus said, "Peace be unto you: as the father has sent me, even so send I you." Then in verse 22 he did a remarkable thing. The bible says he "Breathed" on them and said "receive ye the Holy Spirit." I believe this was the regeneration or born-again experience of the disciples here. This exact thing is what happens to every man when we got born again. In John 1:12 it says, "But as many as received him, to them gave the power to become the sons of God, even to them that BELIEVE on his name." Wow! When you and I as men received Jesus, and BELIEVED upon his name, we received the power to BECOME the sons of God. The word power here is translated as The right, the privilege, and the authority. The word BECOME comes from a Greek word *ghin'-om-ahee* which means to generate or to come into being or to bring into existence or beget. Just like Adam in Genesis 2:7, our Intimacy with God as men gives us the capacity to "Come into being" what God has originally intended us to BE. Without Intimacy with God NO MAN has the ability to become (Identity).

The Intimate Voice

Before we move on to solidify the Destiny part of "The *Blueprint*", I must deal with us as men and our ability to hear and follow the voice of God. Before we finish this chapter, I will give you four principles for developing intimacy with God as Father, and these will help to build your faith and help to develop your inner man to discern God's voice. Another important quote the Lord gave me, and you will hear it throughout this book is "The most dangerous Man in the world is a Man that cannot hear the voice of God." Why is this? Well, when a Man cannot discern or hear God's voice, he will make decisions that not only are detrimental to his success but also to his family and everyone connected to him. In light of this, let's look at another picture in scripture that gives us an example of the importance of a man hearing and obeying God's voice. In Genesis 3:8-11 we see an occurrence of the man Adam and his response to God's voice after the fall *"And they heard the voice of the LORD God walking in the garden in the cool of the day: and Adam and his wife hid themselves from the presence of the LORD God amongst the trees of the garden. And the LORD God called unto Adam, and said unto him, Where art thou? And he said, I heard thy voice in the garden, and I was afraid, because I was naked; and I hid myself. And he said, who told thee that thou was naked? Hast thou eaten of the tree, whereof I commanded thee that thou shouldest not eat?"* This clearly shows Adam had a consistent fellowship or intimacy with God. Even after committing high treason in the garden, God as father is still reaching out to him, still communicating with him. The problem here is that Adam is now filtering God's voice through Fear and you and I were not created to live in the realm of fear, we were created to live in the realm of Love. This entire fear based decision making Adam is doing was all based on Words that came from another source. It's absolutely important that we as Men prioritize developing an ear to hear our heavenly father. Our life depends on it, our marriages depend on it, our families, churches, communities all depend on our ability to hear and obey God's voice.

Communication Equals Intercourse

There was a science fiction movie named *After Earth* made in 2013 starring Will and Jaden Smith. In this movie, the father and son duo were shipwrecked on a now quarantined and dangerous Earth. The main beacon for communication was destroyed during the crash to earth and Cypher's (Will Smith) legs were broken, so he had to send his son Kitai Raige (Jaden Smith) to find the tail end of the ship where there was a backup beacon. The part that intrigued me the most about the movie was the fact that while his son was out searching for the backup beacon that would help them communicate with Nova Prime, his only means of survival was his ability to follow his Father's (Will Smith) Voice. In like manner, our ability to function at our God given capacity as Men is directly proportional to our ability to hear and follow God's voice.

In the book of Genesis, Chapter 3:1-6, we see what we call the "Fall of Man". Eve is subtly and cunningly distracted and lured by the deception of the enemy. She has intimacy with the enemy through conversation. This is so important when it comes to words, because scripture teaches us in 1st Corinthians 15:33, "Be not deceived; evil COMMUNICATION corrupts good manners." We quote that verse, not knowing the fullness of what it's saying. The word communication is a word that means companionship, or even better, intercourse. When you look at the verse with the original meaning, it states that when we are communicating we are having intercourse! That's what happened to Adam and Eve; she was deceived because she continued to allow Satan to plant seeds into her mind through communication and dialog. As a result of this intercourse the bible says she SAW that the tree was good for food. Have you ever been communicating with someone, and in attempting to be clear in the dialog they said to you, "Do you SEE what I'm saying"? This is what happened here: this communication with Satan became so vivid and clear she could SEE what he was saying. His words became an inner image on the inside of her that produced the desire to partake of the tree. Then, the scripture says, "And it was pleasant to the eyes and a tree to be desired to make one wise", so she took it, ate it, and then gave it to her husband that was right there with her while all of this was going on, and the bible says he also ate. This communication with the enemy caused a desire within her that made her take, eat, and then give to her husband. She literally received his words, believed his words, and then conceived his words. All this is found in Genesis 3:6. What does this have to do with hearing God? It has everything to do with it. Notice in verse 7, how both of their eyes were opened and they knew they were naked and they sewed for themselves fig leaves and made THEMSELVES aprons. Right after this event they hear God's voice differently now! They seek to hear Him as Father, but Now because of this intimacy with the enemy, their ability to hear God was hindered. Two things happened in these verses. One, they make for themselves aprons. If you look up what that means, it's the word loin belt. In the book of Ephesians 6:14 the loin belt implied TRUTH. This means that after becoming intimate with the enemy, it separated them from God's voice so the man had to learn how to develop his own perception of truth. God's word was no longer truth to him, truth was now filtered through his sensory mechanism and instead of living from the inside out (governed by God's word and walking in the Spirit), the man starts living from the outside in (governed by circumstances and walking in the flesh) He now began to live in pride, when he previously lived by faith. Secondly, when a man falls from his intimate walk with God, his entire family falls with him. Notice in Genesis 3:8 the bible says Adam (the Man) and his wife hid from the presence of the Lord. Previously they walked and lived in the realm of love, now they are hiding in fear. When a man leaves the love of God and faith in God, his entire family will follow because that's the authority he gave the man. Hearing God's voice as a Man is the highest priority, because faith comes by hearing God's voice. (Romans 10:17)

Back to Destiny

Now let's see the destiny part of this with Adam. It's amazing to see Adam's capacity. God intimately creates him in his image and likeness, gives him complete authority and responsibility over the work of his hands, and places him in the garden called Eden. Now Eden represents *fullness*; it actually translates as *Voluptuousness*. The garden was an environment of limitless potential. Adam was given responsibility to Protect and to keep the image of that garden. Adam also was responsible for giving Identity to every living creature including his wife (Genesis 2:19-23). Clearly, we can see the *Blueprint* in the life of Adam. He was intimately acquainted with God (*Intimacy*), we see God made him in his image and likeness *(Identity)* and finally we see Adam operating in his *(Destiny)* by giving Identity to every living thing and ruling over the works of God's hands Genesis 1:26-30.

Developing Intimacy with God as Father

In conclusion to this first chapter of the book I would like to briefly discuss *Principles for developing intimacy with God as Father*. I will not attempt to teach doctrine, but I will highlight four solid areas a Man can use as tools to draw closer to God. Scripture teaches in James 4:7 that if we "Draw nigh to God; he will Draw nigh to us." To draw nigh is to approach or to get close or near to. Here we see God is not in the business of rejecting his children, so if we do our part by applying and putting into practice principles for developing (intimacy) with him, then we will have a lifetime of discovering who he is. Out of our intimacy with him we then discover who we are (Identity), and out of discovering who we are, we then can confidently walk in every gift and talent and assignment He has created us to fulfill (Destiny).

The Law of First Place

Luke 4:1-4 "And Jesus being full of the Holy Ghost returned from Jordan, and was led by the Spirit into the wilderness, being forty days tempted of the devil. And in those days, he did eat nothing: and when they were ended, he afterward hungered. And the devil said unto him, if thou be the Son of God, command this stone that it be made bread. And Jesus answered him, saying, it is written, that man shall not live by bread alone, but by every word of God"

The number one way to develop an intimate relationship with a person is to make an investment in getting to know them. In our efforts to truly know God through a close personal relationship with Jesus, we must discover through his word principles and processes that point us to him. Studying God's word is the first and foremost priority of any disciple. The word disciple in its original meaning is a word that can be defined as; one who adheres to his master's instruction and make them his conduct for living.

In Luke Chapter 4:4 Jesus was being pressured by the enemy during his forty day fast. When Satan challenged him to submit to his hunger and turn the stone into bread, "...Jesus answered him, saying, it is written, that man shall not live by bread alone, but by every word of God." This verse establishes that if a Man is going to be effective as a Man he must establish that God's word must have first place in his life. A Man isn't truly a Man if he is not living by God's Word. As a Man, studying God's word daily will be the foundation for developing an intimate, personal relationship with God through Jesus. Understanding that God and his word are inseparable will establish within you a mindset that without the word it's impossible to know God. In John Chapter 1:1-3 the scripture teaches "In the beginning was the Word, and the Word was with God, and the Word was God. 2 The same was in the beginning with God. 3 All things were made by him; and without him was not anything made that was made." Look at how the scriptures say God and his word are one and the same. Therefore, it is imperative that a Man be a student of God's word, in order that he may be intimately acquainted with him.

In 2Ti 2:15, Paul is instructing his spiritual son Timothy concerning his responsibility to make the word of God first place in his life "Study to shew thyself approved unto God, a workman that needed not to be ashamed, rightly dividing the word of truth". Notice he said studying God's word shows you approved. This can actually be translated as "Timothy, when you study God's word you display or exhibit yourself as irreprehensible or beyond reproach". God's word has the ability to get into the heart of a Man and deal with his weaknesses and develop character in him. Find a Man that has true character and walks in integrity, and you will find a Man that has given God's word First Place in his life.

The Law of Meditation

Timothy 4:15-16 Meditate upon these things; give thyself wholly to them; that thy profiting may appear to all. Take heed unto thyself, and unto the doctrine; continue in them: for in doing this thou shalt both save thyself, and them that hear thee.

The word "meditate" comes from a Hebrew word, Hagah; which means to murmur, to ponder, to imagine, to mutter, to speak, to utter. The Greek word is, mel-et-ah-o which means to take care of, to revolve in the mind, to imagine, to (pre) meditate. Meditation is a tool God has given us, whereby we may transform our thinking and our self-image. Whatever you meditate on you will SEE and seeing is believing. Every Man is where he is right now because of how he sees himself. A Man can never rise above his Image of himself. Paul again is teaching his spiritual son Timothy about this "Law of Meditation". He tells Timothy that when he meditates God's word and gives himself completely to that word, he will then profit, and his profiting will be evident to everyone around him. The word "Profiting" speaks of progress and advancement. When a Man is stagnant and is not moving forward in his life, it is due to him not meditating God's word and giving himself completely to it.

Another example of meditation is called "Chewing the cud" Certain animals are called "Ruminant" and the word ruminant is from the Latin word *ruminare*, which means to chew over again. There are about 150 species included in this group of animals that "Chew over again", and the Cow is one of them. What the Cow does is chew the grass, regurgitate it from his stomach back into his mouth, and chew and re-swallow into another compartment in their stomach. This is a visual picture of us as believers taking and thinking over the word of God and then putting that word in our mouths by speaking it out. This is the process of meditation.

Our last example of meditation is "Revolving it in the mind". Just think how a rotisserie machine works; it gets the whole chicken cooked well! When we allow God's word to revolve in our thinking it goes beyond our mental capacity, it gets down in our hearts and becomes a part of us. That's what Proverbs 23:7 means when it says "as a Man thinks in his heart, so is he", a Man is a direct reflection of what he thinks about or meditates on.

Meditation empowers our DOING muscles. Joshua 1:8 teaches us "This book of the law shall not depart out of thy mouth; but thou shalt meditate therein day and night, that thou mayest observe to do according to all that is written therein: for then thou shalt make thy way prosperous, and then thou shalt have good success." A Man's success in life is directly proportional to what he meditates on; If he meditates on God's word he will grow in his intimate walk with God, he will develop discernment to hear God's voice, he will be successful in every area of his life, but if he meditates on lust, failure, anger, fear, or any other negative thing he will become what he thinks about the most.

The Law of Prayer

Luke 11:1 Once Jesus was in a certain place praying. As he finished, one of his disciples came to him and said, "Lord, teach us to pray, just as John taught his disciples."2 Jesus said, "This is how you should pray:

Let's start off by defining prayer. So many people think they are praying when they come before God with complaints and worry, but that's not prayer, that's simply "complaints and worry". Then some believe when they bow their head in reverence and in silence and think about some words in their head they are praying; that's not prayer at all that's "thinking". Prayer is simply believing what God's word says about you and or your circumstance and coming before God petitioning him based upon his promises.

Here are a couple of verses to help you better understand prayer. 1st John 5:14-15 says "And this is the confidence that we have in him, that, if we ask any thing according to his will (Word), he hears us: And if we know that he hears us, whatsoever we ask, we know that we have the petitions that we desired of him." According to these verses, a Man is truly praying when he is praying God's will and God's will is his word!

Now that we have established what prayer is, let's look at the prayer life of Jesus, because there is absolutely no better example to use when it comes to prayer like Jesus. His lifestyle of prayer, exemplified through scripture, gives every learning Man a clear picture of what it is to be "A Praying Man". In Luke 11:1-2 the prayer life of Jesus was evident and impactful, so much that the disciples wanted to pray like him. Let's look at some of the examples of Jesus in scripture to help us as Men glean what it takes to be a "Man of Prayer"

1. Before making major decisions as a man he prayed. Luke 6:12 and it came to pass in those days, that he went out into a mountain to pray, and continued all night in prayer to God. Luke 6:13 and when it was day, he called unto him his disciples: and of them he chose twelve, whom also he named apostles;

2. Prayer was a priority and a lifestyle for Jesus. Mar 1:35 and in the morning, rising up a great while before day, he went out, and departed into a solitary place, and there prayed.

3. Jesus absolutely depended on the father in prayer. Hebrews 5:7 who in the days of his flesh, when he had offered up prayers and supplications with strong crying and tears unto him that was able to save him from death, and was heard in that he feared; Hebrews 5:8 though he were a Son, yet learned he obedience by the things which he suffered;

4. Jesus taught that men should pray. Luke 18:1 and he spoke a parable unto them to this end, that men ought always to pray, and not to faint; Amplified version says it more clearly, "Also [Jesus] told them a parable to the effect that they ought always to pray and not to turn coward (faint, lose heart, and give up)."

As part of our development in our Intimate walk with God, we have the responsibility of not just hearing what scripture says about Prayer, but there is an equal responsibility to act on what you've heard. James 1:22 says "But don't just listen to God's word. You must do what it says. Otherwise, you are only fooling yourselves". As Men, we can extract some powerful truths to make us more effective. Make these a part of your lifestyle and your Intimacy with God will increase level after level.

a. Pray before making decisions.

b. Prayer must be a priority and lifestyle.

c. Prayer exhibits our absolute dependency upon God.

d. When a Man quits in his Prayer Life he will quit in every other area of his life.

The Law of Confession

Hebrews 3:1 Wherefore, holy brethren, partakers of the heavenly calling, consider the Apostle and High Priest of our profession, Christ Jesus;

When looking at the word *profession* we can misunderstand it and think that its speaking of your occupation. Some confuse it with what some religions do when they have committed sin, and go to a priest and *Confess* their wrong. In actuality, this is a Greek word that has its root in a word *homo-ol-og-eh-o*. It comes from two words, *homo* that means the same and *logos* which means word. When these two words are put together they mean to *say the same thing;* other places in scripture the same word is used but translated in our English language as *confession.* This scripture can be read more like this, "Wherefore, holy brethren, partakers of the heavenly calling, consider the Apostle and High Priest of our confession, Christ Jesus." I like what one man of God said, "Your profession is your Confession".

There is so much to say concerning "The Law of Confession", but the main idea of it is that we fully agree with God's word in thought, speech and action.

In Luke chapter 4:1-14 we see Jesus "Confessing" God's word during the scrutinizing or temptation of the enemy. *"And Jesus being full of the Holy Ghost returned from Jordan, and was led by the Spirit into the wilderness, being forty days tempted of the devil. And in those days, he did eat nothing: and when they were ended, he afterward hungered. And the devil said unto him, if thou be the Son of God, command this stone that it be made bread. And Jesus answered him, saying, it is written, that man shall not eat by bread alone, but by every Word of God. And the devil, taking him up into a high mountain, shewed unto him all the kingdoms of the world in a moment of time. And the devil said unto him, all this power will I give thee, and the glory of them: for that is delivered unto me; and to whomsoever I will I give it. If thou therefore wilt worship me, all shall be thine. And Jesus answered and said unto him, get thee behind me, Satan: for it is written, Thou shalt worship the Lord thy God, and him only shalt thou serve. And he brought him to Jerusalem, and set him on a pinnacle of the temple, and said unto him, If thou be the Son of God, cast thyself down from hence: For it is written, He shall give his angels charge over thee, to keep thee: And in their hands they shall bear thee up, lest at any time thou dash thy foot against a stone. And Jesus answering said unto him, It is said, Thou shalt not tempt the Lord thy God. And when the devil had ended all the temptation, he departed from him for a season. And Jesus returned in the power of the Spirit into Galilee: and there went out a fame of him through all the region round about."*

Many Men fall into the trap of the enemy and say what they see. They rehearse their circumstances over and over and all this does is bring depression, oppression, and defeat into their households. I read a quote by another man of God and he stated, "if you are a man and you're losing your job or your home, don't sit down with your wife and children and feed them defeat! Grab your wife and say 'Baby, we are moving into another home and I have an opportunity to walk through a new door because my previous door closed, let's get excited for what the Lord is doing'". See, that's agreeing with God, scripture says Our God will supply all our need (Philippians 4:19). That's the Power of Confession.

One of the most powerful stories in the Bible that exemplifies The power of confession is found in 2nd Kings chapter 4:8-37. There was a Shunammite woman who served the prophet Elisha. She made a room for him whenever he would pass by and she fed him. She served him so well that one day he asked what she would desire. He discovered her husband was an older gentleman and she had no child, yet the prophet called her to his door and spoke to her that she would have a child in the time of life and she conceived. One day the child began to cry out that his head was hurting. His father sent the boy to his mother, and he laid on her knees and eventually died. She called for her servants to take her to the man of God, and her confession while headed there was "All is well". Even when Elisha saw her from afar and sent Gehazi his servant to see if she and her husband and son were well, she responded "All is Well". The end of the story is that the prophet Elisha raised her son from the dead, but the main thing as Men we want to extract is that her confession, even when her son was dead, was "All is well".

In Developing Intimacy with God through a personal relationship with Jesus (The Word), as a Man we must daily build within ourselves an image of faith and dependency upon God' word by praying and confessing God's word until we see ourselves, our families, our circumstances the way God sees them.

What's up Man of God?

I'm so blessed to be a part of your journey into biblical Manhood.

This has been my journey for my entire life! The four principles we just discussed are principles that will be a part of your personal development for your entire life as a Man of God. I remember years ago when I first began to understand this, and I would meet other men whether they were saved or not— it didn't matter to me. I just wanted to sit and have a conversation with them because I knew no matter what race or ethnicity or educational background they had, we had something in common and that was being a male. One particular encounter with a man that became a regular way of greeting men for me was when I first started my business. I ended up hiring a gentleman part time, and when I went to his house to pick him up I greeted him by saying "What's up Man of God?" I will never forget the way he looked at me. His face just dropped, and he had a very puzzled look on him. Later after greeting him like that numerous times, he said to me, "PC, (That's short for Pastor Claude) when you first called me a Man of God, I didn't know how to respond because I knew I wasn't living right." He then let me know he had grown accustomed to it and later got born again. All I was doing was acting like my father! After discovering Manhood from a biblical perspective for years, I only could see in him what God sees, and that was A Man of God. I was pulling his potential out of him. Since then, all these years later, I greet every Man with that greeting. As men, once we become truly significant, we can see the significance God placed in others, that's the power of *The Blueprint*. I hope by now you can See *The Blueprint* is not just something I came up with. We have looked at it in the life of Jesus in John 7:29, we have also looked at it in the life of Adam. These are just a couple to start us off with. We are going to look at more evidence in God's word with other biblical examples that reveal "The Blueprint" in further chapters. I am confident what you have learned thus far has caused your faith to stand up on the inside of you and you are excited about taking your rightful place. We are just getting started, let's keep going. Each chapter will provide another brick so you can properly lay your personal foundation as a Man of God.

CHAPTER 2

FATHERHOOD AND ITS ROLE CONCERNING MANHOOD

MALACHI 4:5-6

*"Behold, I will send you Elijah the prophet before the
coming of the great and dreadful day of the LORD: And he
shall turn the heart of the fathers to the children, and the
heart of the children to their fathers, lest I come and smite
the earth with a curse."*

Discovering the Root

There I was, frustrated with my Life. Investing countless hours in prayer and wondering "is this even worth it". I just returned from Jackson, Mississippi, where my wife and I were asked to help develop an urban outreach ministry together with a number of other Gospel rap artists. While living in Detroit, Michigan, in a decent apartment and a decent job, we were asked to be a part of this urban team to reach the streets of Jackson and we did just that. We had seen some powerful things happen during that time. Eventually there were some doctrinal disagreements with us and the people who asked us to come to Jackson, and we were asked to change what we taught or to leave, so I decided to stand my ground and leave peacefully.

After returning back to Michigan we had to stay with my mother-in-law until we could get our own place. Eventually we found a 2-bedroom flat apartment in Adrian, Michigan and we moved in it. I'm now over 30 and feeling as though I've made some terrible choices and they are greatly impacting my wife and children. Consequently, because of this we barely had money for rent and utilities; 3 meals a day was a luxury! THE ONLY THING I HAD LEFT WAS MY faith in God, so I turned to prayer. After some considerable time in prayer, the lord visits me and says to me "I'm going to show you the main root to everything teenagers were going through". This was groundbreaking for me because I was a traveling gospel rapper and a resigned youth pastor, and reaching youth was my strongest passion. When the Lord began to speak to me he said, "Do research on the connection between Fatherlessness and the problems teenagers are facing today."

At that time I didn't even know if there was a word called *Fatherlessness*, I thought I was the only one that heard of this word. It was so fresh to me I had to start researching to make sure I was hearing from Jesus. When I began to research suicide, teenage pregnancy, incarceration, anger, fear, homosexuality, lesbianism, poverty, and more, I began to see the staggering connection between Fatherlessness and these issues. One article that I read stated that, "Some fathering advocates would say that almost every social ill faced by Americas children is related to Fatherlessness". I then coined these social ills as what I call *The fruit of Fatherlessness*.

I brought this out because it's necessary to understand that just like these things are the product of Fatherlessness, in like manner the issue with Manhood is directly connected to a son not having proper Fathering. Therefore, it's absolutely impossible to discuss the issue of Manhood without addressing the *Epidemic of Fatherlessness.*

The body of Christ lost one of its greatest leaders that ever existed a few years back, his name was Dr. Myles Munroe. His last conversations he had was while he was eating at a table with a couple of people. He was talking about the word Patriarch and how it was related to Fatherhood. Dr. Munroe said "Only a Father can make a Man" and then he said, "Here is an even greater mystery: only a Father can make a woman". This statement shook me out of my seat because I had been saying this statement for years, and preaching about Fatherhood since 2003, and here was one of the most prolific teachers, writers, and leaders in the body of Christ saying it word for word! Tears fell down my face and dropped on my iPad as I mourned the loss of such a great patriarch of faith.

I'm so grateful for the impact Dr. Myles Munroe made while here on this earth. He is still fulfilling his own words pertaining to legacy, because there are many of us who valued his wisdom and knowledge and he continues to live through us.

Empty Your glass

Often, we confuse Maleness with Manhood. It doesn't require anything for a person to be Male; just be born Male". As I said earlier, I have a men's ministry I've developed called "The Turn Challenge", and it's a discipleship program exclusive to the development of Men of all ages and backgrounds from a biblical perspective. Generally, when we start our first session I use a concept I gleaned from an old movie from the eighties called *No Retreat, No Surrender*. In the movie, there is a young man who loves kung fu and his dream is to be mentored by Bruce Lee the greatest kung fu fighter of all time. One evening he has an encounter with Bruce Lee, and Mr. Lee asks if he wants to learn from him and the young man says Yes with great excitement. Then Bruce Lee raises up two glasses and says, "This glass represents what you know pertaining to kung fu, and this glass represents what I will offer you as far as my knowledge of kung fu, and for me to pour my glass into yours you must first empty your glass."

That line in the movie never left me, because it paints a perfect picture of what is necessary for us as men to move from ideas concerning our Manhood we have learned from this fallen world system, to understanding Manhood from a biblical perspective. We must empty our glass first pertaining to most of what we have learned concerning our Maleness, so we can maximize our full Manhood potential. When we first start The Turn challenge I tell the Men "Empty your Glass" they say, "But Pastor I'm a man". That's all some of these men have left to hold onto. I recall one young man gripping my hand tight in a handshake after his first session and saying to me with much passion "Pastor, I am a man?" I put a question mark there because when he stated it, it was with no confidence that he was a man, it was with question! Sometimes we have to empty our glass and renew our mind concerning Manhood in order that we might receive something fresh and new that can enable us to experience God's best for our lives.

Give Me Five Dollars

This reminds me of a time when my wife and I were driving in her car together. I stopped at our bank and pulled out some money because I wanted to be a blessing to my beautiful wife. I had already given her some money, but she had been asking me for another twenty dollars. I took the money out of the ATM, but I didn't let her know what I was going to do. I said "Rosie, do you have five dollars?" She said "Nope." I said "baby, I'm trying to bless you, give me the five dollars." She wouldn't let go of that five dollars for nothing, man. I just laughed and eventually I said, "I have twenty if you give me the five." She quickly gave me the five dollars and I gave her the twenty. Well, what did that have to do with anything? My point was: just like my wife needed to trust that I had something better for her and let go of what she had so she could be blessed with more, sometimes we as men must let go of some of our concepts concerning Manhood in order that God show us how he sees us as Men!

I ask every individual in the program (Turn Challenge) to drop their perception of Manhood, empty their cup, give me their five dollars (figuratively speaking) so I can pour into them Manhood from a biblical perspective. Once we settle that I then tell all the men present *We all start off at the same point*: we start as Males! Then I begin to show them the process God gave me.

The Process

When we first start the *Turn Challenge* we all start as Males; here is how God gave this *process* to me: Males are born, but Manhood is developed. The potential to be a Man is already within every Male. For a Male to achieve Manhood, he must first submit as a Son to a Father. Remember, Fatherhood is the highest level of significance because only Fathers can give *Identity.* Then, Manhood is the qualification to becoming a Husband and only Husbands can become Fathers! The Father shapes and molds a son through example of his personal lifestyle, experience and relationship with God as father.

It's important to note that Fatherhood is not something that can be fully realized outside of a close personal relationship with God as Father through Jesus, and we must also understand the Manhood dilemma we are facing is directly connected to our understanding of Fatherhood from a biblical perspective. Now let's look at this "Fatherhood-Manhood" connection and how it relates to our potential as men.

The Fatherhood/Manhood Connection

It is absolutely impossible to discuss Manhood without first discussing Fatherhood.

In order that we may realize Manhood from a biblical perspective, we must first identify Fatherhood from a Biblical perspective. It's like attempting to understand the apple without the apple tree. The fruit is the product of its source, which is the tree, and if we are going to understand Manhood we must understand its source is Fatherhood. Fatherhood is the highest level of significance and only Fathers have ability to give identity. You will hear me repeat this statement throughout my book and I must hammer this into your head until everyone reading gets this in them! I know we are living in a very liberal age where feminism is at an all-time high. Women's equality has sprung up, and now half the time men are feeling so inadequate due to our modern age philosophies of what a Man is, and what a woman is, and what is the definition of marriage or of family. These concepts are warped, and most people know that they are. Even most women know something is not right! Trust me, women are going to love this book, because the burden of trying to be something they are not will be relieved from them as they embrace what God's word has to say about Manhood.

Just under five years back, I remember getting enrollment papers for my youngest daughter. As I was filling the enrollment forms out, I saw something that shook me to the core: I noticed that at the head of household line they had the mother instead of the father. As a faithful husband and a faithful father, I was enraged because I saw exactly what the enemy was trying to do. He is attempting to get the Male Man completely out of the way. He knows that to get the man out of order is to practically destroy the family.

Let's look at God's first dealings with his son Adam when it comes to scripture. Before God as Father gave him any known responsibility, He made him in his image and in his likeness (Genesis 1:26). Often when we look at this text we automatically see us in the equation. We see WE ARE MADE IN HIS IMAGE and WE HAVE DOMINION but one day the Holy Spirit said to me "Son, that scripture is not only about you being made in my image and likeness and you having Dominion. That scripture is about me as a loving Father giving Identity to my Son." This revelation caused me to look at the first 3 chapters of Genesis in a whole new way. I began to look at it from the perspective of Fatherhood. Now instead of seeing it the other way around, it helped me to see that having a clear understanding of what it is to be a Father from a biblical view gives us the foundation from which we discover and build true Manhood.

The Origin of The Word: Father

The word *Father* is the first Hebrew translated word in scripture and it by definition means;

A progenitor, chief, one who begets, a principle, one who brings something into being or brings something into existence. Again, *Fathers can only give Identity.* This is in no way me trying to sound chauvinistic or overbearing and misogynistic. This is a cry to all who are reading this book to finally come to a place where we can get things in order, and divine order starts with the Male Man. We will discuss the issue of divine order in further chapters.

The Father and His Functions

When I began to look at this word *Father* years ago I discovered something so profound. I discovered the same Hebrew word father was given to three different offices; those offices were *the priest, The Prophet* and *The King.* This discovery was amazing. At that moment, while meditating this discovery, I could see the great potential of every Father. Let me explain here what I mean. **57**

A priest represented himself and the people before God; he would go in the presence of God and minister to lord. A prophet had the ability to hear and to see. Some Old Testament translations call the prophet a *Seer* after hearing God's voice and seeing what God desired, as a prophet he came back and spoke what God said to the people. A king had the responsibility to govern and rule God's people. They were sovereignly in control, having final authority.

This lets us know a Father functions in fullness when he operates in all three offices. Every Father has the ability to be *intimate* with God as priest, then as a prophet he can hear and see and give *identity* to a generation and finally as a king, a father has final authority in his home to determine the *destiny* of his family. If we as Fathers begin to function like this, we would save our sons and daughters from experiencing most of the mess they go through. Also, I want you to notice *The Blueprint* when it comes to Fatherhood.

After getting this understanding, I then drew the conclusion Fatherhood is not something that can be achieved outside of a relationship with God as Father through Jesus. It is impossible for a man to be a Father without being born again. Recently, I and one of my Leaders were traveling to Toledo, Ohio, to do an interview on this subject of Fatherlessness and its connection to the problems we have with understanding our Maleness or Manhood. During this conversation The Holy Spirit spoke through my friend, pertaining to the scripture found in John 15:5 where Jesus is teaching that he is the vine, we are the branches, we are to remain in him and he in us, and as we do this we are able to produce much fruit. Then he said something profound, he said "For without me you can do NOTHING!" Wow! This scripture just permeated our hearts as we were driving because it says exactly what the Lord said to me pertaining to Fatherhood, Manhood or anything for that matter. Without Him we can do absolutely nothing, we can't be Fathers without Him because Fatherhood is something that is exclusive to a close, personal, intimate relationship with Jesus. We can't be Men without him because Manhood is something that is exclusive to a close, personal, intimate relationship with Jesus. This is where our problem is: we have to see the Fatherlessness epidemic and the lack of understanding of our Maleness or Manhood as a spiritual problem that cannot be solved with natural resources! Again, without Jesus we can do nothing! Jesus is our way to the Father, back to God's original intention for Man. We must settle it in our thinking that a Father can't function effectively without knowing God as Father. This was the case with Adam. God as Father took the time to create a Man in his image and in his likeness before he gave him responsibility. God being the totality of what Fatherhood is, made the man like Himself. Based on this, we see God's original intention was that Adam be a Father like himself. It was God's intention that Adam function in all three of these areas; *Priest, Prophet* and *King*.

The Misunderstanding of Fatherhood

Psalm 127:1 Except the Lord build the house, they labor in vain that build it: except the Lord keep the city, the watchman wakes but in vain.

This scripture shows we have the ability to build without God! Oftentimes most men come out of their mother's womb into families Fatherless. Some are raised by men who never discovered what it is to be a Father. We grow up and believe that just because we had sex with a woman, and she gets pregnant, and we bring this child into the earth, then that act makes us a Father. This is the misconception that is leading to the breakdown in society we are seeing. Just because one plants a seed doesn't make him a Father; A Father is one who not only plants a seed but brings it into being what it was originally intended it to be. If we are going to see men reach their full potential as a Man, then we must embrace Fatherhood from a biblical perspective. Just like when building a house, you must first begin with the foundation, and the foundation of the family is the Father. If our concept of Fatherhood is wrong then the whole entire family will be out of order.

I believe this is why we are seeing so much happening in our families today. Families are so disconnected, so desensitized to all the wrong that is going on. Our sons have lost sight of what it is to be a Man. Our daughters have lost sight of what it is to be beautiful and lady like. Most of them are tough and rugged and competitive with their husbands. The workplace has become a priority, career has become a priority, and now families don't even sit at a table and discuss their day together. We make excuses for it and say, "This is a different time we are living in", but the truth is we must take a careful look at the direction we are going. We must reconsider and evaluate where we are as families.

The Father and His Family

In the first chapter I discussed the whole understanding of what it means to *Restore* something. I mentioned that to restore is to bring something back to its original state or movement back to the point of departure. When looking at the very first family we can get God's mind on how he sees the family. God first starts with the Male Man. He places this Male Man in the environment of his presence and then gives him his purpose and destiny. Then he gives that Male Man a wife who is called by the Male Man a *Woman* a man with a womb. The Male Man and the Woman were to come together and have children. Clearly, we can see the family structure starts with the Male Man, and if we get that out of order then the entire family will be out of order. Now I know we are in a time where we have what we call "Blended families." Since the fall of man and the decline of the biblical image of what family is supposed to look like, today we have diverse pictures of what family looks like. According to studies there are 6 different family structures, but we will talk about seven.

1. The nuclear family; this is the traditional family consisting of a father, mother, and their biological children.

2. The single parent family; this is those who care for their children without the assistance of the other biological parent.

3. The step family; this family structure is recognized due to over 50% of all marriages ending in divorce.

4. The Grandparent family; this family consist of grandparents raising their grandchildren. There are many reasons why this family unit exists.

5. The childless family; this family is often referred to as the forgotten family.

6. The extended family; this family consist of two or more adults who are related by blood or marriage living in the same home.

7. Same sex family; two individuals of the same sex living together and raising children.

Though we have diverse family structures, we must recognize God's original picture of family. The Nuclear Family Structure has been attacked from the very beginning of creation. It was always God's intention that the family is the source for shaping culture, but today we see the very opposite happening. It seems culture is shaping family and because of this our families are deteriorating! The enemy knows the family structure provides the basis for our moral code. He also knows the only way to get to the family is to get to the marriage, and the only way to get to the marriage is to get to the Male man! Again, the Male man is the foundation of the family and when he is out of place the family cannot withstand the storms of life. The family structure is also an environment for children to grow and become what they were created to be. God's answer to heal the hurt in humanity is still the family! Psalm 68:6 says "God places the solitary in Families." If you look at the penal system, you'll discover that 70% of youths in state operated institutions come from fatherless homes, and 85% of all youths in prison come from fatherless homes. These young men that have been incarcerated all have the same thing in common: they all lacked the love and structure family provides, and most will say they were raised without the love and support of a father. The father and the family he builds provides Gods originally intended image that would cause a young man to grow and become great. I'm reminded of the story of NFL Player Michael Oher. He was born May 28th, 1986 in Memphis, Tennessee. He came from a broken home and his estranged father was murdered while Michael was in high school. Sean and Leigh Anne Tuohy became Michael's legal guardians, and he developed into a college football star and a top NFL draft pick. The environment of the Tuohy Family provided the love and the structure necessary for Michael to grow and develop his gifts and talents. I strongly believe that without that family environment where a father was there as the foundation, we would not know the Michael Oher we know today. Just like the verse in Psalm 68:6 states "God places the solitary in Families." There are Millions of Michael Ohers out there; in our country alone, there are 24.7 Million children that are fatherless. This is why it's impossible to discuss the problem concerning Manhood without recognizing its connection to fatherhood. Again, Fathers— and only Fathers— can give Identity! I am going to really bring this out so you can have clear understanding in my chapter on "The Authority to give Identity."

The Affirmation of a Father

Matthew 3:17 "And lo a voice from heaven, saying, this is my beloved Son, in whom I am well pleased."

It is said of a daughter that the first man she falls in love with is her Father. When a young lady doesn't have a true Father figure in her life she will look for that missing element, that emptiness, that void, to be filled by other men. On the other hand, it is said that a young man spends his entire life looking for the approval of his Father.

I can attest to this, growing up without a father who knows and loves God in your life as a young man leaves as much of a deficit in a young man's life as it does in the young lady's life. When Jesus was speaking to his disciples about his departure, he said he was going to go away but he would send them the comforter. He was speaking of The Holy Spirit. In verse 18 of John chapter 14 Jesus said, "*I will not leave you comfortless.*" This word comfortless means to be *Fatherless* and this word has many other translations, but the one I want to bring out is the word *Bereaved.* The word bereaved speaks of the grief, the pain and the loss one experiences when someone you love dies or passes away. When I began to meditate on that, the Holy Spirit revealed to me that *Fatherlessness* leaves the exact same imprint on the mind of a child as death does! So many young men are walking around just merely existing. No purpose, no hope, no dreams. These young men have no value for life because they have been QUIT on! People are asking every day, "What can we do to stop the violence in our inner-city streets?" Well, the answer is that we as fathers must stand up and begin to reach out to these young men as if they were our own sons. We must begin to be a father to the fatherless. The absence of a father in the life of a child can affect a child for a lifetime.

Every child was created with a need to be loved and affirmed by their father. It is every little child's desire, after working hard at school, to come home with their grade card and say "Dad, Look at my report card". Every young man, while playing on the football field or on the basketball court, looks out to see if his Father is there and to see that proud look on his face. I remember being in one particular high school, and let's say his name was Nathan just for privacy sake. Nathan was a star quarterback for the football team, and he was also a star guard for the basketball team I was on. I remember he had such confidence, even his smile was confident, and I noticed that every game his Father was there cheering him on, believing in him. His father was his biggest fan. Nathan was radiant with courage and I knew him personally, so I will never forget the effect it had on me just seeing his father there every time, dependable and predictable. I looked him up a while ago on social media and noticed that even to this day Nathan is doing very well. He is very successful, and that success is directly connected to the strong affirmation of his Father.

Fathers must affirm their sons! Recently my wife and I were in conversation with a mentor of ours. I would say he is close to 60 years of age. This powerful man of God has the Love of God just oozing from him. When he comes into a room you feel safe. He doesn't come across tough and overbearing, nor does he come across weak and intimidated. He comes across with what I call "The Love of a Father". He is strong yet sensitive, he is honored and yet humble. He is the epitome of what a Father should be like. While in my conversation with him he said to me, "Pastor Bevier, I spent my whole life waiting for my Father to tell me who I was", That amazed me, because when I look at him he is a Man that I look to, in my mind he has it all together and I would have never thought he would experience something like this. He also went on to say his Father called him to come over one day and finally looked at him and said "Son, you are a Man's Man". My mentor said that after hearing those words from his Father, he just broke down and cried. Here is a Man at the age of 60, still in need of the love and affirmation of a father. After our conversation His words penetrated my very being because I too have done the same thing. I silently wept on the phone because the affirmation of a Father in his son's life is so valuable that without it a son can go his entire life with that missing element. This is exactly what happened in the scripture above. Before Jesus went into his wilderness experience and endured the antagonistic thoughts and assaults of Satan during his time of temptation, Jesus confidently walked towards his destiny empowered by these words, "This is my beloved son, in whom I'm well pleased".

The "Tough Guy" Image and What It Produces

Most young men who never experience the Love and affirmation of a Father grow up very hard and tough, and they build this impenetrable wall around them to protect them. If we are truly honest with ourselves as men, we would say that this mindset comes from insecurity. My personal definition for insecurity is to secure oneself inwardly. This insecure self-image we create as men causes us to build walls that so called "protect us", but the problem is it also keeps every person you need in your life to help you at a distance from you, where they can't assist you at all. This deficit concerning the affirmation of a Father is what many young men have missed, and due to missing out on this they perpetuate the same thing.

Here's a great example of this. In 1974 a Folk-Rock Song was written by a prolific songwriter by the name of Harry Chapin. The song was called "Cat's in the Cradle". It became a Number 1 hit song and topped the Billboard 100. The whole message in the song was about a son craving the affirmation and attention of his Father. The Father was so busy he didn't have time for his boy when he asked to spend time with him. The son would say hey dad, let's spend time together and the Fathers reply would be "Son I'm too busy". Then the son said, "Hey Dad let's play Ball together" but the Father would reply again and say, "Son I'm too busy." Years would pass by and the tables would turn, and the son eventually grew up and started college and he came home. His Father had by this time grown old and life had slowed down for him, and now looking to spend time with his son he said, "Son let's take some time together" but now the son was too busy and just asked his Father for the car keys so he could go. Throughout the song the son keeps saying "One-day I'm going to be like you dad, you know I'm going to be like you." This is a true but very sad depiction of the condition of most of our Father Son relationships, and this has been the cause of the breakdown of Manhood. When I would hear that song growing up, I recall thinking that this was something the Father deposited in his son and now he's reaping it.

Because of the lack of Love and Affirmation from Fathers, men have become so tough, harsh, and insensitive. We have adopted this mindset that the more disconnected from people you are, the more of a man you are. The problem with this way of thinking is that as a man it follows us home, and we haven't mastered how to disconnect from it, so we treat our wives and children in the same manner. This is what the songwriter was trying to convey.

The Man Kiss

I just got done worshiping in an awesome atmosphere of God's presence; there are hundreds of us there in the sanctuary and the peace of God is so powerful. I'm open and vulnerable to his voice, his instruction; whatever the Lord desired to do, I thought I was ready. At least that's what I Thought! It's in my opinion the most important day of honor on the planet and that day is Father's Day. It's probably in the mid 1990's and we are honoring our Pastor for being the great spiritual father that he was, and his children came up to the stage and something absolutely foreign happened and it almost took the breath out of me. My Pastor's oldest son walked up to him and when he had finally approached him he then reached down and kissed his son! And when I saw it, from my chest went chills down through my entire body as I wept uncontrollably, because not only have I never experienced a moment like that with a Father, I also didn't know that kind of affection from Father to son existed.

One of my Pastor friends operates like this with his son. Daily he kisses him and looks him in his eyes and tells him he loves him. This is the important role a Father plays in a young man's life. A Father must treat the heart of his Son as a garden and realize whatever he plants, that's what's going to grow. If the father plants love, trust and confidence in his son's life, those are the things that will grow up in him. Then when he is married he will have those things richly planted within him and he also will be able to convey them to his children.

A Father Expels Fear

This is what the Apostle Paul was doing in the life of his spiritual son Timothy. In 2nd Timothy 1:7 we read a very familiar verse of scripture. Paul tells Timothy we have not been given a spirit of fear, but of power and of love and a sound mind. One day I read that and saw that verse as a Father teaching his son not to fear. I knew then that fathers help their sons and daughters to overcome the obstacles of fear in their lives so they can achieve greatness. The other side of the coin is that whatever fear a father doesn't overcome; he will project on his children.

I had a similar experience with God. One day, I had some personal issues I was battling and every time it seemed that I overcame it, that issue popped its head right back up in my life. Therefore, during prayer one day the Lord said to me "Claude, you are not just battling your own issues, you are battling the weight of past generations". Well I didn't quite know what that meant until I began to discover from God's word what he was speaking to me. Thank God for his word. It has an answer to every dilemma we will ever experience. All we have to do is find it in his word and stand on it, and there is enough power within his word to bring itself to pass (Read Isaiah 55:11).

One day I was musing through the word and saw this verse in Exodus 20:5 ""Thou shalt not bow down thyself to them, nor serve them: for I the LORD thy God am a jealous God, *visiting the iniquity of the fathers upon the children unto the third and fourth generation of them that hate me"* WOW! I now understood what he meant, there were doors opened in Generations before me, doors of disobedience and disorder from my forefathers. This was the weight of past Generations I was fighting. I often tell my congregation "I Became a Man at the age of Thirty-Two". Most would say "No Claude you are legally a man at 18 and in some states 17". My response to them is that age doesn't make you a man; the acceptance of responsibility makes you a man. At thirty-two I set my mind that I wouldn't blame the death of my fathers for my lack of maturity, I wouldn't blame anyone else in my life for my lack of maturity. I am where I am because of my decisions. That day God was able to speak to me about what I was allowing as a man to remain in my life, and I have learned that whatever I don't resist has the right to remain! In that moment I knew that as a Father, whatever doors I wasn't willing to close would permit issues to rightfully visit my children.

Here is another verse that makes it clear; found in Lamentations 5:7 it says, "Our Fathers have sinned, and they are not, and we have borne their iniquity". My God! What a responsibility: a Father has to live a Life that is exemplary of God's love and grace. As fathers we must not just live for ourselves. We have generations in us. Our obedience or disobedience will determine what our children and grandchildren will have to face. Some would say "Pastor Claude, we are in Christ and we are Blessed and free from any form of the curse" however, ignorance in any area of God's word gives access to the curse! We must learn to cooperate with God the Holy Spirit and allow him to lead and guide us into all truth; truth concerning what it is to be a Father from a biblical perspective, because whatever doors of disorder or disobedience we don't settle will have the right to visit our children. My love for my Children and grandchildren has been a consistent motivation for me to Change!

Like Father/Like Son

Genesis 5:3 "and Adam Lived a hundred and thirty years, and begat a son in HIS OWN LIKENESS, after HIS IMAGE; and CALLED his name SETH."

It has always been our Heavenly Father's intention that Fathers *know* him *intimately*. The highest level of Significance is Fatherhood because only Fathers can give Identity. Here we see Adam now removed from the presence of God (Genesis 3:22), fallen from God's original intention for him, without divine assistance from his heavenly Father, still trying to function as a Father. Notice Seth is made in the Likeness of his Father (Adam) and in his (Adam) Image. Adam is in the worst state he has ever experienced. He is in confusion and chaos separated from God as Father and source. One of his sons in this fallen state of confusion and chaos kills the other brother. This state of confusion has now affected the whole family. The bible states in Genesis 4:25 that Adam knew his wife again; and she bare him a son, and in this confusing state Adam names his son Seth. Well ok, nothing seems wrong about this until you dig just a bit deeper. The Nobse Study Bible list and Jones' Dictionary of Old Testament Proper Names agree: That the name Seth means Appointed. His name is indicative of what the state of mind both Adam and eve were in. When you look up the word TUMULT it is defined as; a state of noise, commotion and confusion. It is clear that Adam in his confusing state projects on his son his personal experience in his time of separation and confusion.

This account of Biblical history is repeated throughout scripture, and even now in our current society. It also is an example of our inability to Father without God as Father! We must buy into the Biblical view of Fatherhood to be effective Fathers and give proper identity to our children because their Destiny depends on it.

The Three Mentalities

Hebrews 6:12 "That ye be not slothful, but followers of them who through faith and patience inherit the promises."

In keeping with the role a Father plays in the development of a Man's life, we must carefully look at this verse. The first thing I want you to see is that I call The Bible "The Man's Book." Often in Church we see most responsibility delegated out to women due to the lack of stable, faithful, reliable, and dependable Men! We as men must start seeing that this "Church Thing" is a "Man Thing." One of the reasons we don't see many men is because during the dark ages, men were sent out to war and the priests had to learn to make church a relevant thing for the women and their children while the husbands were off to fight. Somehow it seems we are still recovering from that time.

Often in Churches you rarely see men in the forefront taking the helm and leading the way. Most young men don't have very many men or Fathers to reference in the local church. Just recently I was reading another article entitled *"Christianity is short of Men."* It said the typical congregation in the USA draws crowds that are 61 percent female and 39 percent Male. It also stated that on any given Sunday there are 13 million more adult women than men in our Churches. It stated the majority of Church employees were women and that on a Sunday 25% of married women would worship without their husbands in attendance. This clearly states that we as men have to change our thinking pertaining to our role not just in the local church but in society as a whole, because the next generation of Male Men need a point of reference as to what it means to be a Man. Now in all fairness, I want to say men are coming up in every area of church. I am under a world-renowned Pastor in the Chicago Area and the minute you hit the parking lot you see strong, courageous men serving their local church. I just wanted to make clear that we are overcoming as men in Jesus name.

I want to extract though three mentalities from this verse and I believe it's going to help you. These mentalities are the result of young men having no point of reference or having a Male figure that doesn't understand what it is to be a Father from a Biblical perspective.

The Bastard MENtality

The first thing the writer says is that we should not be *Slothful*. The word slothful is a Greek word *no-thros'* which means to be lazy or sluggish. What's even more interesting is that this word is derived from another Greek word *noth'-os* which means to be a spurious or illegitimate son, or a *Bastard*. The word *Bastard* means simply one without a Father. Now this is powerful because we are in a time where men don't like to work or be responsible. There are more men today living with women, sitting home and doing absolutely nothing. Spending hundreds, even thousands of dollars the woman earned on video games and shoes and clothes. Now don't get me wrong, I'm not pointing fingers or trying to bring anyone down, but as men we are not going to be able to change anything unless we can recognize there is a problem. This attitude and mindset is one of slothfulness. As a business owner I have had opportunity to hire multiple young men. They would ask for a job, get their first paycheck and then you wouldn't see them for a while. No call, no show, you wouldn't hear from them for a couple of days. Again, this is a slothful mentality and it is born of Fatherlessness. Let's look at this from a biblical perspective because God has never intended that anyone be fatherless. I personally believe Fatherlessness is the number one Epidemic in the world, and if we can change it then we can absolutely change the world. Notice the next thing he says is we should be "Followers." Now I'm going to tie two mentalities together, but first let's see what the writer is saying. He's stating we should always have someone that we can look up to and emulate their lifestyle. The man that has the bastard mentality says, "You never were there for me, you hurt me,

I don't need you," and this is how they respond to every male figure that tries to lead them or give them any instruction. They live their lives blaming everyone around them for their failure. The bastard mentality also takes on the anger and the hatred that momma has because the male figure wasn't there, so when a young man is raised by her, her hurt and wounds become his. Now he has developed an excellent mindset toward what hurting women want, and he never really grows or experiences maturation when it pertains to manhood. He simply will not trust a male figure, so he becomes the next mentality.

The Baby Boy MENtality

As I said earlier, the bastard mentality won't submit, follow, emulate, or learn from any man because he doesn't trust a man. The problem is that only Fathers can make a man, so when he gets married he doesn't know how to be a husband because he never arrived at manhood, so he doesn't marry a wife, he looks for his momma in a woman. She takes care of him, washes his clothes, cleans up after him, and pays his bills, why? Because that's the only way he knows to treat a woman because the bastard mentality tells him you can't trust any man, any boss. any pastor, any leader. The only young men that break out of these mentalities are those who find a mentor or father figure. So me yo ung me n wh o ar e fatherless overcome it because they love sports or some program so much and the sport or the program has a Male figure running the program. The person can break it because the coach has leverage because of the love they have for the program. If you will carefully study, you'll find mothers who are raising their sons by themselves can raise some awesome young men if they partner with coaches, pastors, and community leaders that help to fortify male qualities and structure within them. It is absolutely imperative we establish and settle that "*Only Fathers Can Give Identity*". This is why the writer in Hebrews 6:12 says "be ye Followers of those who through faith and patience inherit the promises of God." As men, we need

Fathers that we may emulate. We need Fathers that no matter how successful they are, they are able to come down to the level of their son, their protege' and help them achieve greatness. I'm so thankful I have that in my Pastor. He takes the time to pour into his spiritual sons and help to develop us with God's word.

The Broke MENtality

To finalize this verse in Hebrews 6:12, The last Mentality is the broke mentality. Statistically it is said that Children in Fatherless homes are almost four times more likely to be poor. In 2011, 12 percent of children in married-couple families were living in poverty, compared to 44 percent of children in mother-only families. (*Source; U.S. Census Bureau, Children's Living Arrangements and Characteristics; March 2011, Table C8. Washington D.C.; 2011.*) When a young Man grows up Fatherless and resist the instruction of Male Men that can resource his life, poverty is the consequence. On the other hand, when we are open to being fathered and willing to follow, we then have access to what's on the life of the one that is fathering us. In the case of this verse, the writer says we should *follow* and this word follow is a Greek word which means to *act or pretend to be like* those who through Faith and patience inherit the promises of God. Those who truly embrace sonship will walk in The Blessing and Favor that is on the life of the one they are following. As I mentioned earlier in this book, my life was greatly impacted by my submission and surrender to the Male figures that were in my local Church. Those influences changed me for the better. Another great example of this is found in 2nd Kings chapter 2:1-14, where we see the prophet Elisha following his Mentor the prophet Elijah. During this time Elijah consistently asked Elisha to remain back a few times, but Elisha would respond by saying, "as the Lord lives and as thy soul lives I will not leave you." In verse 8 we find Elijah and Elisha standing by the Jordan, Elijah took his Mantle, wrapped it together and smote the waters, and they were divided so that both of them went across on dry ground. What's amazing about this story is that his relentless pursuit of following the prophet Elijah brought him to a place where in verse 9 Elijah asked Elisha, "Ask what I shall do for you, before I be taken away from thee." And Elisha asked for a Double portion of the same spirit that was upon him. As the story goes, Elijah went up by a whirlwind into heaven and Elisha cried out "My Father, My Father, the chariot of Israel and the horsemen." Then he saw him no more. After this occurrence, Elisha rent his clothes in two pieces. Then he took up the Mantle of the Prophet Elijah, and stood at the bank of Jordan, and smote the waters, and said, "Where is the Lord God of Elijah?" And when he smote the waters, they parted just like they did for the prophet Elijah. This is a perfect example of why we as Men need other Men to "Follow," we must have those whom we may see as examples for living so that we may use as a point of reference concerning Manhood. We must be able to receive the "Mantle" of those whom we are following.

"Transgenerational Thinking"

It's sad to see the breach that we have between generations. It seems that this whole epidemic of Fatherlessness has created a barrier between one generation and the next. The transfer of the mantle of Elijah to Elisha is what I call "A Transgenerational Blessing," I remember again hearing some of the last words of the late Dr. Myles Munroe, where he talked about one generation passing the baton to the next generation. A Baton is a short stick, used in a race, that is passed from one runner to the next. He discussed how he had a dream or a vision of an individual in a casket, and he held a baton tightly in his hands as if he did not want to let it go. I remember hearing him say that there was a problem with one generation passing the baton or mantle on to the next generation. As I thought of that, I began to also reflect on how the successive generation of young men have lost trust in following the previous generation, and this too has created this breach. We must again, as Malachi 4:5-6 says, "Restore the hearts of the Fathers to the children and the hearts of the children to the Fathers." Then the barrier between generations can be healed and the baton or mantle can be passed from one generation to the next. Like Elisha received "The Transgenerational Blessing of Elijah," As a young Man learns to trust and follow, he too can experience the blessing and favor that is upon the life of the individual he is following. This has been my case. As I continue to follow my Pastor and the leaders that God has placed in my life, Their Anointing, wisdom, favor, and blessing have all come upon my life, Family, and Ministry.

The Responsibility

In conclusion, pertaining to the role of a father in the development of Manhood, we need to understand that the highest calling and most important role in life is not to be a 5-fold minister, businessman, president, or anything else; the highest calling and most important role in life for a Man is Fatherhood! WHY? Because again, *"Only Fathers can give Identity."* I believe with all my heart that every issue in society can be traced back to this whole Fatherlessness epidemic. I got the awesome opportunity to watch a great Christian movie entitled *The Case for Christ.* The movie was based on the true story of Lee Strobel, a young man who was a brilliant journalist, highly educated but fully atheist. His wife had an encounter with God's Love and got born again. He then began to do research to prove that this whole Jesus thing was just a hoax. Every doctor, scientist, and intellectual individual he went to weren't able to give the concrete evidence he was looking for to prove Christianity was false. Faye Dunaway played the Psychologist he went to last. After hearing his questions and concerns to build his case, she asked him a profound question: "What is your relationship with your Father like?" He answered her but didn't understand the nature of the question. Then she responded by asking him if he was familiar with some of the most prominent atheists such as Hume, Nietzsche, Sartre or Freud. He then responded by saying to her that these individuals were some of his greatest heroes. Then she said something that took me out of my seat, literally, while I am watching the movie. She said, "Did you know that all of them had a Father who either died when they were young, abandoned them or was physically or emotionally abused, in a world of therapy it's called a "Father Wound". WOW! Each of them had absent or abusive Fathers and this created a hurt that caused them to think a certain way about God as Father. I was then even more fired up, because now I understood the root to the atheist belief system was also Fatherlessness. This helps us to understand the massive responsibility we have as Fathers and as Men.

CHAPTER 3

THE FOUR LEVELS
OF INTIMACY

MATTHEW 22:36-40

*"Teacher, which is the most important commandment in
the law of Moses?" Jesus replied, "'You must love the lord
your God with all your heart, all your soul, and all your
mind.' This is the first and greatest commandment. A second
is equally important: 'Love your neighbor as yourself.' The
entire law and all the demands of the prophets are based on
these two commandments."*

Vertical and Horizontal

These first three chapters have been strategic. We first covered
the importance of a man's Intimacy with God as father. This
Intimate relationship with God as Father is the first and foremost
important relationship, because it determines the success any
man will have with others. I'm reminded of the time when Jesus
told Peter he would deny him. Peter does what every man does
and that is to respond from his inflated ego, "Lord not me, I'll
never deny you". Jesus responds and says to him, "Peter, Satan
desires to sift you like wheat but I have prayed for you that
your faith doesn't

fail". Now watch this, Jesus did not pray that He (Peter) wouldn't fail, because Jesus knew Peter in and of himself would fail! He prays for his Faith or his intimacy with God not to fail. Then he says when you are converted, strengthen your brothers. This scripture paints a picture that all success in horizontal relationships is a product of our vertical relationship with God. In the second chapter, we covered the importance of the role of a Natural Father or a father figure when it comes to Manhood. Remember, only a Father can make a man. There must be Intimacy between Father and son. This means a man must be accountable to someone. Your accountability can be with your natural father, a pastor or a spiritual father, a coach, or a businessman. You must have someone you can learn from and glean from to realize your manhood potential. No man is an island unto himself!

Now in this chapter we are going to deal with what I call *"The 4 Levels of Intimacy."* These levels of Intimacy deal with our connection and companionship with one another as men and with our spouses, children, and other relationships. In my dealings with and mentoring of young men and grown men alike, I have discovered each man generally has a level that he is on when it comes to intimacy. Here is what I mean if you were to gather a group of men together and put them in a room with each other, you would find they are all on different levels as far as their connecting and openness to one another. I've noticed in our men's meetings that there can be different races and ethnic backgrounds gathered together but even though they are physically there most men have a hard time connecting. This lack of intimacy is growing rapidly today, especially when it comes to millennials. The reason is that in previous generations families communicated physically and verbally. Activities were done together like going to parks, fishing, and other family outings. I'm not saying all families have abandoned the tools for connecting, but if you were to just closely observe where we are today by taking a walk downtown in your city or just driving and looking at those who pass by in their vehicle you would notice most people are glued to social media. Today people are taking selfies, smiling and immediately after the picture they wipe the smile off and go back to depression and anxiety. Point being is that social media is replacing real intimacy with people. Most people today don't know how to act without their device. I read an article about this generation that said when a young person is hurt or fears something, they don't run to a physical person to get consoled, they run to social media.

Understanding this and all the busyness of life and its impact on men of today gave me the desire to locate men by determining what level of intimacy they were on. I paid close attention to the mindsets of men over a period of time and separated the mindsets pertaining to intimacy into four different levels. This gave me the ability to identify where each man was. These levels of intimacy did not come from a textbook or someone else's reading material. They came out of my personal time working with other men.

Love, the Determining Factor

The greatest determining factor when measuring a Man is his ability to love God, love himself, and love others. As a matter of fact, most men grew up never hearing the words "I Love You" so in turn they have a hard time expressing love with others. So many men grew up with what I call "*A Love Deficiency*". A deficiency is when you lack something or it's absent in your life.

Due to this Love Deficiency, Men don't have it to give to their wives or their Children, so this Deficiency perpetuates in the bloodline and it continues so unchecked that even after death it follows the blood line. Look at what Lamentations 5:7 says "Our Fathers have sinned, and they are not and we have born their iniquity". This verse is saying my concept of Manhood not only affects me, but it also affects everyone that is connected to me.

The way a man sees himself or understands himself will be the way he sees and understands others, including his spouse and children; again, this is called *The Law of Projection*. A man will always see others through the filter of his own significance, and nothing else! Jesus gives you and I as men the solution to this Love Deficiency, He says "Love God", but wait— it's impossible for me to give what I don't have, so how can I love God? Well Jesus solved that also, The Holy Spirit by the pen of John wrote in 1st John 4:19 "We Love him because he first loved us". Romans 5:5 teaches us "The Love of God is poured out in our hearts by the Holy Spirit that is given to us".

With these scriptures, we can clearly see we as Men receive Love from God, and when we welcome that Love we then have Love capacity to Love ourselves with, and then we can Love others (our wives, children, family, friends) with that same Love.

A Man who has no Love capacity will always stay reclusive and isolated, and when a Man isolates himself, he hinders not only his personal development but also his entire family. Man of God, always remember that *Isolation will always result in Amputation.*

Discovering the Level of Association (Connection based upon common interest)

Definition: connection, a relation resulting from interaction or dependence.

Ephesians 4:15-16 "He makes the whole body fit together perfectly. As each part does its own special work, it helps the other parts grow, so that the whole body is healthy and growing and full of love. Instead, we will speak the truth in love, growing in every way more and more like Christ, who is the head of his body, the church."

Men have such an ability to be right in a room with everyone in there, but yet not be "All the way there". Men love this level of Intimacy because we all commonly as men start here. On this level we control the narrative; we let people know about us only what we want them to know. We tell it like it is based on our view, how we see it. Our view may be incorrect but on this level, it really doesn't matter because at the end of the day we take the mask of "I got it all together" off! We determine the people that we will allow to go to the next level with us when we are here. This is the level where you connect with people because you have something in common. Maybe as men you both like sports or maybe you both collect antiques, maybe you both like old cars. I don't know what the common interest is but we all have them.

I remember myself and others connecting based upon the common interest of Gospel Hip Hop. I was a Gospel rapper and so were they. Our common interest brought us together, but it was our willingness to be accountable to one another that still keeps us together. Because of this strong accountability with each other, we now are raising our children together and a part of the same church and leadership team I happen to pastor. Our relationship had to grow through these intimacy levels so we all could be where we are today.

The Power of Discomfort

In our men's program the *Turn Challenge*, one of the 1st things I do is connect men with other men in the program that they don't necessarily feel comfortable with. As men we need to learn that the presence of discomfort doesn't mean you shouldn't engage with others. In moments of discomfort there are most likely some very valuable lessons learned. Discomfort also is a sign of growth, and here's what I mean. When lifting weights, it can be absolutely uncomfortable at first, but the more you consistently lift the more you are rewarded because you can see your growth levels. However, if you feel discomfort and quit, you will never grow. Sometimes in relationships we feel discomfort as men, and then back away instead of consistently working at it so we can get better and grow. The danger in this mentality is that on the other side of discomfort is your next level, and every level has a reward.

For an example, one particular year I went to a conference and the guest speaker was a world-renowned speaker, author, writer, and philanthropist. He was seated at a certain table and across from him was another guest speaker, who happened to be a millionaire. When I came through the doors a good friend of mine grabbed me, took me right up to the front and sat me down at the table between these two awesome giants in the faith. During the service I was completely fine until we were asked to stand, hold hands, and pray. I'll never forget the feeling that came over me. I began to wonder, "does my breath smell?", I thought something was crawling in my hair, my palms were sweating, and I was so upset with myself in that moment of discomfort, I was so nervous I couldn't even connect in prayer. Shortly after the meeting was done I went back to my hotel and I questioned the Lord why that happened to me. His answer was this: "In the presence of greatness inadequacy and inferiority will always surface". That statement from the Lord reminded me of what I learned years ago as a young man concerning gold when it is being purified. I was taught that the heat from the fire causes the impurities such as dross to float to the top, so the goldsmith can scrape it off and look in the gold to attempt to see his reflection or image. This is exactly what is supposed to happen when we as men hold each other accountable, and sometimes it feels uncomfortable when it seems someone is in your business, but it's for your own good. God sometimes will allow a man to experience discomfort because he is trying to get the things out of us that may be preventing us from winning in life.

When a man fights accountability it generally is due to that man having a Love Deficiency. Because of this, men stay withdrawn. Association is the level that gives men the ability to connect without seeing each other's differences. This common interest connection will draw Men together but it won't keep them connected. If walls aren't removed, then it's easy for a Man to allow insecurity to set in. The definition of insecurity is "lacking self-confidence or assurance", but I have my own definition and it is: IN-SECURE-to secure oneself inwardly. This is when, through fear, a Man keeps others out of his life.

Let's get really frank here! This is extremely dangerous because God didn't create us as men to be independent. When we do this we are placing our confidence in Man and not God (See Jeremiah 17:5). Secondly, God never created us to be self-dependent because then that's pride. God did create us to be God dependent and interdependent. This is a must, because we are seeing men walk out on their marriages and families by the droves. Men are tired, giving up, and quitting on life, and the reason why is because as a man, you can't do this thing called life on your own. Find someone that will hold you accountable and love you enough to tell you the truth. Also, sometimes you just need some brothers you can kick it with. Sometimes men just have to set some things up where you can refresh yourself as a man, just go have fun. Find some other brothers and find some great connecting tools such as football games, basketball games, Church functions, or going out to eat with one another's families. These kinds of activities build connections and help you move as a man to the next level.

As a connection is developed, it's then important to get out of your comfort zone and take your accountability to the next level, because in the first stage of intimacy men are still guarded. Things remain hidden in this stage. A Man must grow and develop by moving to the next level of intimacy to secure that he won't remain in isolation. Another reason this is important is because all a Man's horizontal relationships with others are a direct reflection of his vertical relationship with God. No Man can say "I love God" but has a problem with loving others! 1st John 4:20 says "If someone says, 'I love God,' but hates a fellow believer, that person is a liar; for if we don't love people we can see, how can we love God, whom we cannot see?" So, there must be some accountability through connection where other Men are allowed into your life, where common interest can create an environment of reciprocity that permits growth for all involved.

The Level of Communication (Sharing)

Definition: the activity of conveying information.

After connecting based upon common interest, our next level of Intimacy is communication. This is what I call the *Level of Sharing.* As Men, sometimes we don't even want to talk a lot, let alone open ourselves to other men. Because of some of the misinformation again we've learned as Men, we often think communication is a sign of weakness, but this is far from the truth. So many marriages and families have been utterly destroyed due to lack of communication. I read a book years ago, and recommend it to all men to read. This book was written by the late Dr. Edwin Lewis Cole entitled *Communication, Sex and Money.* In his book he alluded to the fact that Communication, along with sex and money, were the main areas that cause struggle in marriages. Therefore, in like manner, the lack of communication with those who can help you can prohibit you from maturing, developing, and becoming what you were created to become, and ultimately it can hinder you from fulfilling your purpose.

"Isolation will always result in Amputation." Wow!!!! This quote has the exact same impact on me now while writing this as it had when he first spoke it to me.

When I think of this quote I think of the many men I looked up to. Some have lost their wives through infidelity; some have lost their jobs, careers, or positions in life due to some character flaw. Some have even lost the respect of family and community due to some personal vice (I will discuss Vices later in the book). When I think about these incidents, I think to myself "If they would have shared with someone their pain, maybe this would have not gotten this far."

I want to make something very clear here: I am not judging any man! I am a firm believer that just the fact we are men places a target on us. Men have been emasculated, effeminized, and have lost confidence in themselves. Most men have grown up in households where being a man meant providing and protecting, but never were taught to love. As I said earlier, most men never heard the words "I love you" while growing up. My wife had to teach me how to open up and say, "I love you." I, like most men, equated those words as weakness until years after being born again. I understand why we as Men are hurting today now more than ever. It is simply my desire to share what the Lord has taught me. These Levels of intimacy kept me accountable and enabled me to overcome my personal vices and weaknesses.

Proper Council Means Accountability

The number one tool God will use to change a man is the tool of accountability. An unaccountable man is a liability on the battlefields of life. God's word teaches us about having proper counsel in our lives. The book of wisdom, or Proverbs, speaks about this "11:14 *Without wise leadership, a nation falls; there is safety in having many advisers*". Also, look at Proverbs 15:22 *"Plans go wrong for lack of advice; many advisers bring success"*. Therefore, as Men we must allow the walls of fear and lack of trust to come down and share with one another. In Genesis 4, after Adam committed high treason in the garden of Eden, one of his sons followed his lack of fellowship with God, and instead of being his brother's keeper he became his brother's killer!

Mastering the levels of association and communication enables us as men to see each other as interdependent resources to help each other grow. Another verse in the bible that brings our interdependence out along with accountability is found in Ecclesiastes 4:9-10 "*9 Two people are better off than one, for they can help each other succeed. 10 If one person falls, the other can reach out and help. But someone who falls alone is in real trouble.*" That says it all; when a Man is alone he is "in real trouble". Take this moment right now, shake off the Tough Man mindset and begin to share with others and communicate your issues and circumstances, because you never know who has been strategically aligned to your life to assist you. That's why James 5:16 teaches us to "Confess or (Communicate) our faults to each other and then Pray for each other (not talk about each other,) that we may be healed". It's our communication, sharing, and trusting each other that enables us to get better in life; this is how God intended Men to work together.

Revelation (I see you, you see me)

Definition: to uncover, to make something evident.

Now that we have discussed association, the level where we connect based upon common interest; and communication, the level where we begin to share and trust; we now can move to the level of revelation. The level of revelation is where connecting and sharing has given each person access to one another's lives. At this level you become familiar with one another, and strengths and weaknesses are exposed or uncovered. A good example is when a man meets a woman he likes, and they connect with each other, then they begin to share and communicate. They date, spend time together, go to the movies and out to eat together. Pretty soon she visits his apartment, she sees his clothes lying around, and then she starts telling him how to clean his house; now things are getting uncomfortable. This continues and eventually they are around each other enough to see the weaknesses. They used to say a statement like "That's too close for comfort." At this level of intimacy most people quit on each other, because without God's love humanity has been wired with a narcissistic type of love where everything and everyone must be centered around our lives. Consequently, when other people's weaknesses begin to be revealed, people generally lose interest because their problems may slow us down. This again is why so many marriages fail— because when the parties involved begin to see that the other individual is in the process, a lot of times that person's process conflicts with the other's. Again, this is selfish because the truth is, we all are in the process and though we all are striving to be like Jesus, we still are working on us. Can the Church say Amen? There is only one thing that will help any relationship continue to develop and move forward on this level, and that is God's Love.

1st Peter 4:8 says "Most important of all, continue to show deep love for each other, for love covers a multitude of sins". This word used for love here is "Agape"; it describes "The God kind of love". It's a love that pursues you and I beyond our fault. 2nd Corinthians 13:14 message bible calls God's Love an "Extravagant Love". When looking at the word extravagant it means "to be unrestrained and recklessly wasteful." That's how God Loves us, he looks beyond our weaknesses, failures and personal problems and loves us unconditionally.

I have discovered that God has no budget when it comes to how much he loves you and I. This is the kind of love a Man must have in order to develop meaningful relationships. Without God's love a Man can't love his wife, children, and friends properly because when we are without God's love we see each other's faults, and we become selfish instead of being selfless; we look for what we can receive instead of what we can give. At this level of Revelation, a

Man must walk in God's Love and allow it (God's Love) to be a lens through which he looks through, in order to give others the opportunity to grow with him.

Assimilation (Becoming one)

Definition: the process of becoming one.

The final level of Intimacy is Assimilation. This is the level where as a Man you have moved past all the insecurities and lack of trust, and you've moved beyond isolation and withdrawal. God's love has become so real to you that you see yourself and others through the lens of his extravagant, recklessly wasteful love. Now you're settled, confident, and courageous in your relationships, giving others the opportunity to grow and mature without criticism or judgmental attitudes.

Having arrived here is a beautiful place because when a Man is here he can see the best in every person, he can speak well of every person, and he can believe in every person, because of the way he sees, treats and responds to others is out of the way he sees, treats, and responds to himself. This is the highest level, because a confident Man can now be unified in friendships, or any relationship he's in. This is the level where there is no fear because the Man is being perfected in Love (1st John 4:18).

I've used a Man's marriage many times during these 4 levels of intimacy because I believe a Man's marriage reflects his own wellbeing. I learned years ago, that a man's wife is a direct reflection of himself. When you see a Man who loves and treats his wife right, you'll discover a man who has mastered these 4 levels of intimacy.

I noticed that nowhere in scripture will you find God instructing the woman to love the Man. You'll only find that she is instructed to honor and revere her husband as unto the lord. There is a reason why, Scripture teaches the man to Love his wife as Christ loves the Church. Here is what I believe. Women innately know how to love, but sometimes it's hard for them to honor and show reverence due to some of the things that have been taught in society. Men, on the other hand, understand honor and reverence but lack when it comes to love, so God settles it by making the Man the Love Conduit of the family. Remember, The Male man is the foundation of the family, he is the responsible party. God will always start with the head.

God knew the Man would have to submit and honor him to receive love capacity. Now that the man has received God's love he can love himself and his wife properly and packaged within that love is honor and reverence for him. When the children see love, honor, and reverence being exemplified in the home, then obedience for their parents is given. All of this is found in Ephesians 5:21-33 and Ephesians 6:1-3. Notice that Completion and wholeness comes through the Man.

Finally, it's impossible to discuss Intimacy with God without dealing with our intimate walk and relationships with others. Truly the measuring stick of how much a Man loves God is determined by how much he loves, respects, and treats others. This is the Law of love fulfilled.

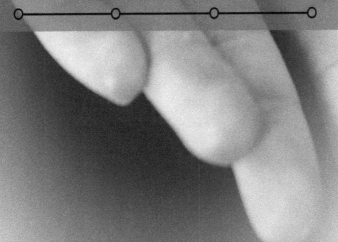

SECTION 2
IDENTITY

The greatest act of a man is the act of becoming, because once a man truly becomes, then and only then does he truly belong.

CHAPTER 4

DISCOVERING THE BLUEPRINT

JEREMIAH 1:5

"Before I formed you in the womb I knew you, before you were born I set you apart; I appointed you as a prophet to the nations."

It's Not Working Correctly

The first three chapters dealt with our Intimacy with God, understanding Fatherhood and its connection to Manhood. Then finally how Intimacy with God affects a Man's way of dealing with his wife, children and other relationships. The next few chapters we will deal with the Intimacy and Identity connection and how it relates to who we are as Men. Who we are has everything to do with our intimate relationship with God as Father. I mentioned earlier in the book that it's impossible for a Man to realize his Manhood potential outside of a close, personal, intimate relationship with God. When a Man grows in his relationship with God, making that the highest priority of his life, then he can see himself as God sees him. All throughout scripture you will see this *Blueprint*. A man knows God, then he can know himself, and that in turn gives him the ability to know what God put him here for. He then can fulfill his purpose on the earth. Again, I call this process of Intimacy, Identity and Destiny *The Blueprint*. I purchased a cell phone for my wife some time ago and when we received it we had no idea why it wouldn't work correctly. I then went to the retail store and they couldn't figure it out either. Then I asked others that had a similar device, and even though they had a similar device they still didn't know how to fix it or make it work properly. Finally, I contacted the manufacturer and from their location they were able to determine the problem and sent me a new one. I literally spent days toiling, trying to figure the issue out with my wife's new phone and then in one phone call to the people who created it the problem was solved. This is how it is with us as men; we look to everything and everyone else for the solutions to our Manhood issues and still come up empty. We must turn to him who made us, he knows who we are, and he knows everything about us.

When reflecting on this I think about the prophet Jeremiah. God created him. He knew his capacity, and he called him to be a Prophet to the Nations; he called him to speak a word that would root out and tear down opposition, and then this word would build and plant God's desires and plans. Jeremiah's image of himself was small, so God spoke to him and said, "Before I formed thee in the belly *I knew thee*; and before thou came forth out of the womb *I sanctified thee*, and *I ordained thee* a prophet unto the nations." Here God uses *The Blueprint* in the life of Jeremiah. The first thing Gods says to him was "I knew thee" (INTIMACY), then he says "I sanctified thee" which means God distinguished him, he separated him, or another definition I found says, I withdrew you from the crowd. Wow! That's IDENTITY. When God says he withdrew you from the crowd that means there isn't anyone like you. Did you know there are 7.5 billion people on this planet and not one has your fingerprint! Glory! The last one he said was "I ordained you a Prophet to the Nations." *Ordained* here speaks of assignment and

Purpose (Destiny). Just like God knew Jeremiah, He knows you and me. He knows every intricate detail pertaining to who we are, what our capabilities are, and what we are here to do. God knows you with such detail that Jesus said, "God knows the numbers of every hair strand on your head (Luke 12:7). This is why it's so important for us as Men to discover our true Identity out of our Intimacy with God. As a result, knowing who we are is the product of Knowing God intimately. This is highly important because as a Man we must find our significance in our relationship with God as Father if we are going to fulfill our Purpose in life. Now let's discover the *Blueprint* in the lives of some of the other Men in the bible.

From Abram to Abraham

Earlier we looked at the life of Adam to discover the *Blueprint* in his life. Now, let's take a look at Abraham, my favorite character in the bible. The story of Abraham intrigues me because I can see myself and so many men in his life. Abraham is called "The Father of Faith", and that title seems so unattainable when you look at it. It's somewhat like so many businessmen or athletes who have achieved so many great things in their lives, that when you look at where they are now it can become intimidating and seem out of your reach as a man to achieve. This is why I believe *The Blueprint* is so vital for men because men are created to dominate and win in life, but when we can't realize what we dream about then that unrealized dream causes us to doubt our value and our worth, that's what the scripture in Proverbs is talking about when it says "Hope deferred will make the heart sick: but when the desire comes, it is a tree of life" (Proverbs 13:12). So, becoming who God created us as men to be is of most importance.

Let's take a journey and see the development of Abraham— the process by which he came into being "The Father of Faith". I think it is vitally important for us as men to relate to the process, because the process is what God used to produce the promise. Again, if you only see Abraham then you don't value the process. Therefore, we are going to spend some time looking at Abram, so we can value Abraham. Metaphorically speaking think every man starts off as an Abram and God gives every man the ability to become Abraham. A lot of times the process is left out because it's not as popular or pretty to look at. It's kind of like the caterpillar becoming the butterfly. There is nothing special about the cocoon and the spinning of the cocoon and that isolated time of transformation, but when the caterpillar transforms and breaks out of the time of waiting and becoming, then we all can see its beauty. Like Abram, every man has the desire to overcome his personal weaknesses and break out and become the best man he can be, but the truth of the matter is that the process is strenuous. This is why I personally like Abram, Scripture exhibits his journey of brokenness and relentless dependency upon God as a man who wants to obtain God's best for his life. Let's talk about it.

The Journey

Before Abraham became Abraham, he was simply Abram! Abram simply means "High Father". This exemplifies his capacity without God. Abram went through this process I call *The Blueprint* and I would like to point this out to you. In Genesis 12:1-4 God calls Abram and requires him to get out of his country, kindred, and from his father's house unto a land he would show him. Based upon Abram's obedience level, God would be able to release the Blessing of a Father to him. Verse 4 states that Abram departed as the Lord had spoken unto him. In Chapter 12:7 God promises Abram he would give the land unto his seed. From Genesis chapter 12 to Genesis chapter 17 we see Abram go through complications in his effort to try to accomplish what God had said unto him. First of all, he disobeys God and takes Lot, his brother's son with him when God told him to leave his Father's house. Also, we see him attempting to assist God by having a son through Hagar (Ishmael). This kind of reminds me of myself and most men. When God's ways don't seem to fit into our timing and planning we come up with our own "Lots and Ishmaels" to try to bring to pass what God promised us.

The problem is that when you look at Lot's name in the Hebrew language you will see that Lot means to *Cover or to Veil* and when we try to assist God through our possible conventional ideas of how we believe he's going to get it done, then we suppress, cover, veil, and prohibit what God has planned for us. We see this concerning Abram and Lot in the book of Genesis 13:5-7 how Abram grew very rich and Lot began to accumulate substance and the land was not large enough for both of them, therefore strife entered in between the herdsmen of Abram and the herdsmen of Lot. After this Abram presented Lot with a solution for the contention: note that when a man has a "lot" in his life it will bring opportunity for strife and contention! Abram's solution was that they part ways and whichever area Lot chose Abram would go the opposite (Genesis 13:8-11). Here is the powerful part, strife and contention in a man's life will cause him not to be able to see God's plan and purpose in his life. In Genesis 13:14 notice what the scripture says: "And the Lord said unto Abram, after that Lot was separated from him. Lift up now thine eyes, and look from the place where thou art northward, and southward, and eastward, and westward: 15 For all the land which thou seest, to thee will I give it, and to thy seed forever." Wow! Notice God spoke after Lot was separated from him. God told him NOW you can lift up your eyes and SEE, meaning Lot's relationship with Abram was preventing him from HEARING and SEEING what God had for him.

I have a Men's program in our church and it's called the "*turn challenge*", it's a ministry developed from this process called *The Blueprint* and one of the things I teach is that "The most dangerous man in the world is a man who can't hear or discern the voice of God." The reason why is because when a man is cut off from discerning God's voice, he will then live a pride filled life, self-dependent and independent of God. This is what happened to Abram: his relationship with Lot prohibited his intimacy with God as Father, and due to that, strife and contention entered in, and in order for Abram to get to his potential he had to give God first place in his life by separating from Lot. I discuss the importance of surrounding yourself with proper relationships later in the chapter called, *The Power of Environment*.

Five Chapters later in Genesis 17:1 the bible says "When Abram was ninety years old and nine, the Lord appeared to Abram, and said unto him, 'I am almighty God: walk before me, and be thou perfect.'" Here we are almost 25 years since God first spoke to Abram and made this promise to him. My question when I first read these passages is "what the heck took him so long?" I can remember hearing all those religious answers others would say like "God is always on time, but he is never early". That kind of thing would burn me up as a man because we want to get it done; we want to accomplish the goal. Just show me what to do and I'll do it. Then I would hear "It's all in Gods timing". Here we go again; none of this was helping me as a man at all.

The Answer Came

One day in meditating these scriptures the Holy Spirit opened my eyes to see what actually happened. I began to see the *Blueprint* again. First of all, Verse 1 says the Lord *appeared* to Abram; this fascinated me because now I wanted to understand what the word *appeared* meant. As I began to dig into it, I began to see that this word *appeared* meant God revealed himself to Abram. Wow, I saw it (Intimacy). Abram here is having a difficult time believing he would be who God said he was and that he would have a son, so God reveals himself to Abram as "the almighty God". The word almighty is a Hebrew word that means to be incapable of being overcome, incapable of being attacked, unshakeable and unyielding. God reveals himself in an Intimate fashion to Abram as the almighty God, and now every limitation is removed from Abram's thinking, he begins to intimately see God bigger than his age, bigger than Sarai and her being beyond the age to have children. Now, Abram no longer sees his wife's inability to produce because he is seeing her through Gods ability to produce. This is why Intimacy with God and/ or his word is our most valuable asset. Through meditation of his word, a man can see his Heavenly father as his source, his strength, and sustainer.

Next, God then takes it a step further in this verse: he invites Abram to "Walk Before him". This is profound because the word before is the Hebrew word *panyim* which means "the presence of the Lord or the very face of God". This is the place Adam and his wife hid from in Genesis 3:7, the presence of the Lord. In that place of God's Presence, that intimate place where he saw God as all powerful, almighty and incapable of being overcome; in that presence God tells Abram "Be Perfect". Wow! Let me explain what happened here. See, as a man by himself, Abram's condition seemed insurmountable, it seemed impossible. However, in God's presence every trace of fear, inadequacy, inferiority, shame, and guilt must be eradicated as if it never ever existed! Again, intimacy with God, in his word, in his presence, hearing his voice is more important than anything else in our lives because it's there in that intimate place where all of our limitations are permanently removed in Jesus name. In addition, the word *perfect* means to be "entire" which means to be complete. A man that doesn't know God intimately is an incomplete man. He's fragmented and broken, and when an incomplete, fragmented, broken man meets a woman he will then fragment and break her because insignificant men cannot see the significance in a woman!

I know this is heavy, but you and I know that only significant individuals can see the significance of others. It's called the "Law of

Projection" At our church we have three Projectors, every service we have announcements and details about upcoming events that have been programmed in the computers, and that which has been programmed can be projected through the projectors. We are never surprised as to what is projected because we programmed everything that's being projected. This is how it is with us as men, we can only project that which has been programmed in us, and if we are broken, fragmented, hurt, or wounded then that is what we will project on our wives, children, and everyone in our circle of influence. How we see ourselves as men will determine how we see others. Therefore, it's hard for insignificant men to celebrate the success of others because they can only see greatness through the filter of their own personal accomplishments. More importantly, then a Man's perception of people, places, and things is his personal projection of himself. We cannot SEE anything or anyone beyond our own self-image. Therefore, it's so important for a Man to intimately know God. His intimacy with God changes his self-perception.

The Law of Projection

God deals with Abram's insignificance because it was how Abram was seeing himself that was prohibiting God's promise from coming to pass in his life. He tells Abram, get your eyes off yourself, get them off of your wife, get them off of your own inability to produce (Abram) and get your eyes on me! I am able to perform what I said I would perform, but I need you to see yourself the way I see you and not the way you see you. In verse 5, God does the next part of *The Blueprint* in the life of Abram. He says, "Neither shall thy name be called Abram, but thy name shall be called Abraham; for a father of many nations have I made thee." Notice that when Abram begins to see God in the place of Intimacy, the very first thing God deals with concerning Abram was how he saw himself (Identity.) He tells him "Stop limiting yourself, stop calling yourself Abram, start calling yourself Abraham!" See, Abram was what he could do without God but through Intimacy with God, Abram could come into being as Abraham, which meant to be the "Father of Nations". Now through his Intimate relationship with God as Father, Abram is given significance, and his name now becomes Abraham.

I must deal with this right here concerning Fatherhood and its role in giving Identity. Fatherhood is the highest level of Male significance because only fathers can give identity. Abram's problem was clearly that he didn't see himself as God (His Father) saw him and it was Abrams intimacy with his Father that changed his self-perception, (how he sees himself). Here's the beautiful thing: there is absolutely no insignificance in God. I love this quote the Holy Spirit gave me years ago, "There lies within the changed the irresistible desire to see others' lives and circumstances changed." Glory to God! Our heavenly Father's desire is that we as sons and daughters come to him, get in his presence, get in his word, and see him for who he is! He is just waiting as a loving Father to tell us who we are. No man has the ability to discover himself outside of a close, intimate, personal relationship with him.

As I said previously, it's been almost 25 years since God spoke to Abram but now things are happening. God is now going to show Abraham what the problem has been with Sarai not being able to bear children. Let's look at this in Genesis 17:15 "And God said to Abraham, as for Sarai thy wife, THOU shalt NOT CALL her name Sarai, but SARAH shall her name be. 16 and I will BLESS her, and give thee a son also of her, and she shall be a mother of nations: kings of people shall be of her."

Let's unlock this now, men! As soon as Abram becomes Abraham (Identity) God tells him "Stop calling your wife Sarai". Why? Because Sarai in Hebrew means dominant woman or to exercise dominion. Do you see what was happening? Abram kept seeing his wife out of his own personal insignificance. That's why he called her Sarai. If you imagine this story you can see Abram blaming his wife for his own lack of success. This is what we as men do. Now, I'm not getting down on us, but the truth is that we as men project on our wives how we see ourselves. We blame shift, and that whole mindset evolves out of seeing ourselves outside of the Fatherhood of God.

Notice that in verse 15, God tells Abraham to call her Sarah because Sarah means lady, princess, or Queen. You and I know it was Abraham seeing himself the way God saw him that caused him to see his wife the way God saw her. This last part is Destiny. We know the end of the story; Abraham and Sarah had Isaac because Abram and Sarai could not have had Isaac! There you have it in the life of Abraham, *Intimacy, Identity, and Destiny*.

From Simon to Peter

Here is another example of *The Blueprint* found in the life of Simon, a Man who got a revelation of who Jesus was and in turn became who God created him to be. In the book of Matthew 16:13-19, there is a phenomenal occurrence with Jesus and his disciples. In verse 13 Jesus asks a question to them "Who do men say that I the son of man am? Verse 14 they respond, "some say you are John the Baptist, some Elias and others Jeremiah or one of the prophets." In verse 15 Jesus says Ok, I know you know what they say about me "but who do you say that I am?" See this is powerful because so many Men are living off of the echo of what someone else said about Jesus, but if a man is going to realize his full potential he is going to have to know Jesus for himself! I love what happens next. Verse 16 says, "And Simon Peter answered and said, thou art the Christ, the son of the living God." Verse 17 Jesus says "Blessed art thou Simon Barjona: flesh and blood hath not revealed it unto thee, but my Father which is in heaven. 18." And I say unto you also that you are Peter, and upon this rock I will build my Church and the gates of hell will not prevail against it." Now, in order to understand this fully you and I have to discuss the word revealed here. This word here is the Greek word "ap-ok-al-oop-to" This word means to take the cover off or to disclose. It paints the picture of something that is there but yet hidden or covered so you can't see it. Jesus said here it was the heavenly Father that gave Simon the ability to see. Now remember we don't see with our eyes we see with our mind. So, let's glue this together now.

Theologically, much has been said concerning the interpretation of this group of scriptures but I think it's pretty self-explanatory. Simon gets a revelation (he sees-intimacy) who Jesus is and then Jesus turns around and tells him who he is (Gives him identity). Now this is so significant because in the verses here, just like with Abram, you see that before Jesus calls him Peter his name was Simon, meaning a reed: this implies instability but when he gets a revelation of who Jesus is, he names him Peter which implies Rock. His *identity* is changed through his *intimate* understanding of who Jesus is. What takes the cake in these verses is that Jesus says this process will enable the Church to be an unstoppable force when it comes to advancing the Kingdom of God *destiny*; He said the gates of Hell will not prevail! This word means hell's forces cannot and will never overpower the person that knows Jesus *Intimately* and knows who they are in him. The entire *Blueprint* is right here in these verses; Simon gets a revelation of Jesus *intimacy*, Jesus changes his name from Simon to Peter *identity*, and finally Jesus said this Church that was built like this cannot be stopped when it comes to advancing the Kingdom *destiny*. Any man that will build his life based upon these three principles *Intimacy, Identity, and Destiny* will realize his full potential.

CHAPTER 5

THE POWER OF ENVIRONMENT

GENESIS 2:15

*"And the lord God took the man and put him into the
Garden of Eden to dress it and to keep it."*

Trading Places

In 1983 Eddie Murphy and Dan Aykroyd starred in a great comedy called *Trading Places*. In this movie there are two very rich brothers that make a bet for one dollar. The details of the bet were that they could take two different kinds of men, one from an impoverished background and another from a very successful background and switch their environments. Based upon this bet the impoverished individual, who was played by Eddie Murphy, would become successful because of the new environment and the successful individual, played by Dan Aykroyd, would become impoverished if environments were switched. Consequently, the bet was true, Eddie Murphy became successful and Dan Aykroyd became poor. This comedy, in my opinion, depicts clearly the *Power of Environment.*

The late Dr. Myles Munroe taught us years ago that fish cannot fulfill their potential outside of water, plants cannot fulfill their potential outside of soil, and birds cannot fulfill their potential outside of the sky. Water is the environment for the fish to become and to realize its potential, soil is the environment for the plant to become and to realize its potential, and the sky is the environment for the bird to become and to realize its potential. In like manner, we must buy into the biblical idea that NO MAN has the capacity to become and fulfill his full potential outside of a close, intimate, relationship with God as father through Jesus. Intimacy with God through his word and his presence is our environment as men so that we may become and realize our potential. Outside of the environment of Intimacy with God, just like the movie *Trading Places*, we as men lose our ability to become who God has created us to be, thus resulting in completely unfulfilled lives.

An Unlimited Environment

We see this environment of God's presence, love, and word in the life of Adam. In the book of Genesis chapter 2:15 it says, "And the lord God took the man and put him into the Garden of Eden to dress it and to keep it." This Garden was the man's *environment*. The word Garden meant to hedge or to protect and the word Eden speaks of *Voluptuous Living* or Living in Fullness. This Garden was an environment for the man to know his Heavenly Father intimately and to hear his voice and to fellowship with him every day. Adam was given the responsibility to *Dress and to Keep* this Garden. There have been some great things said about this Environment Adam was placed in and his assignment given to him, but I would just like to bring a little more light to the picture. When Adam was given responsibility to "Dress and Keep" the Garden, the Hebrew language suggests this meant he would worship, serve, become, and work out the potential placed within him by his

Heavenly Father. For years I just kept seeing Adam with a rototiller kneeling down pulling weeds. Thank G od f or t he Holy Spirit and etymology, because that concept was incorrect.

Adam was not a weed puller; he was God's image and likeness in the earth. Through his Intimate fellowship with the Father he was supposed to guard and protect the image and environment of this Garden. Adam thought like God in every way; Adam at this point as a man couldn't see any limitation because the environment he was placed in was an unlimited environment. Anything was possible. He was supposed to, through intimacy with God, take and enforce what he saw and heard in that environment and carry it across the entire planet. Adam was *supernatural*: he lived above the natural realm, which means he lived above and beyond reason. When I say this, I mean his mindset was exactly like his Heavenly Father's. Adam did not know what healing was, because in order for him to know what healing was, he would have had to know its counterpart, which is sickness or disease. Adam did not know what prosperity was, because in order for him to know prosperity he would have had to know its counterpart which was poverty! Adam only knew what God programmed in him. His responsibility was to guard this way of thinking and live from that perspective. This was the environment of the first man, Adam. When Adam left his environment he fell, and when he fell he didn't fall geographically, he fell in his thinking. When a man gets out of his environment he falls from thinking like God originally intended him to think, and as a result he begins to live like a mere man! The first thing we have to understand if we are going to realize our full potential as men is that It is ABNORMAL for a man to function outside of Intimacy with God. Notice in Genesis 3:9 the lord God called unto Adam and said unto him, "where are you?" Now how does an all knowing, all powerful, everywhere all the time God not know where his Man was? That's the question I asked years ago, but that's not what was happening here. God knew where Adam was, he wanted to see if Adam knew he had left his environment. When

Adam left the environment of God's presence he left his ability to think like his Father, be like his Father, and to fulfill God's purpose and plan for his life. This means when he left God, He left himself. He no longer could be who God intended him to be as a Man without God as Father!

Man of God, we must lose sight of any mindsets pertaining to manhood we have learned from this fallen world system. We must REPENT (change) our thinking as to what a man is and go back to thinking according to God's word. Ephesians chapter 2:10 teaches us "For we are God's [own] handiwork (His workmanship), recreated in Christ Jesus, [born anew] that we may do those good works which God predestined (planned beforehand) for us [taking paths which He prepared ahead of time], that we should walk in them [living the good life which He prearranged and made ready for us to live]." According to this verse if you as a man got born again, you were "RECREATED IN CHRIST JESUS", you are now geographically located in the environment of Christ Jesus. Through Jesus we have access back to God's plan for our lives as men. Now everything we will ever be and everything we will ever accomplish in life has already been prepared, prearranged, predestined, and planned before we even got here. We have access to the voluptuous and full way of thinking as men. In this environment of God's presence and love, we are not just coming up with our own ideas and plans; we are not an island unto ourselves. We are now a part of God's own master plan and purpose, so in order that we may maximize our full potential as men, we must learn what it is to be intimately acquainted with God as our father and allow that to be our environment. We must guard this gntimate fellowship with God above all that we do.

Be What You SEE "The Law of Emulation"

When speaking of the power of environment I must deal with the effects that environment has on a man. Many of us, though we have been born again, recreated in Christ Jesus born anew, still haven't been able to actualize our Manhood potential because of wrong environment. All of us are the product of our environment, things we've experienced, and things we've been exposed to. This means that a Man must choose his environment if he will become all God has intended him to be. There is a saying that goes like this, "Show me a Man's closest friends and I will tell you how far he will go in life." This is also called the *Law of Association*. Whoever you are around the most, you will become like. Think about it, if I wanted to be a star basketball player, then it would make sense for me to get close to Stephen Curry and learn his ways so I could be like him. If I wanted to be a great musical artist, then I would get close to someone like Kirk Franklin or Lecrae and learn their ways so I could be like them. This is what I call "Being what you see"; also the relationships in your life or environment must be relationships you can glean and grow from. I heard years ago one man say "If you are the smartest person in the room, then you are in the wrong room." You must find people that know more than you, that have experienced more than you.

It's fascinating how God as Father created all of us. The book of Psalms 139:14 says we were fearfully and wonderfully made. Our heavenly Father made us in such a way that we emulate what we see! Now we have to understand that we don't see with our eyes, we see through them. When I'm talking about seeing here, I'm talking about seeing with our minds. A man must surround himself with people that challenge the way he SEES things. That's why I love Ephesians 5:2, it tells us to Imitate or emulate Jesus and walk in love even as he walked in love. Glory! We can not only have an environment full of successful others who are instrumental for our life's success, but we can go even farther than that in Imitating and emulating Jesus. When a Man is intimately acquainted with God through giving the word of God first place in his life, meditating on that word through prayer, worship and confessing the word; that man has the ability to SEE differently than the average man.

As a matter of a fact, our intimate relationship with God makes us uncommon Men! The more we see things from God's perspective, the more we become like him in every area of our lives.

Creating an Environment for Transformation

Earlier in the book I mentioned I was a youth Pastor when God first began to deal with me in terms of my understanding of what I call *The Blueprint*. One day sitting at my desk I saw this verse of scripture and it leaped out to me as I studied.

In the book of 2nd Corinthians 3:18 it says "we all with open face beholding in a glass or (Mirror) are changed into that same image from glory to glory, even as by the spirit of the Lord." This verse shows that through our Intimacy with God's word we are transformed into the same image of Jesus. The word transformed or changed, depending on which version you're reading, is speaking of a scientific term of metamorphosis. There are two words put together to make this word. The first is *Meta* which implies association and the second is *morpho* which implies to change or to fashion. It means the more we associate ourselves through intimacy as men with God's word and his presence we are then changed or transformed. This means that when a man doesn't change it's because he is not intimate with Jesus! It's impossible for any man, regardless of upbringing, background, bloodline, education, or anything else; to stay the same once he has developed a close intimate personal relationship with Jesus.

As I mentioned in the chapters that deal with intimacy, prayer, meditation of the scripture, giving God's word first place in your life, and confessing the word all are a part of a man's transformation and change. This reminds me of a caterpillar and its process of becoming a butterfly. The first thing we must understand is that a caterpillar has to create its own environment for transformation. Although the potential to BECOME the butterfly is already within a caterpillar, it must do certain things in order to create its environment to be transformed into the butterfly. The first thing a caterpillar does is it eats! That's right; a caterpillar just goes around eating and eating. The second thing a caterpillar does is it attaches itself to a tree branch or twig or leaf upside down and the third thing a caterpillar does is it spins out of its mouth its own cocoon or chrysalis, which becomes a protective environment for it to become or come into being a butterfly.

Well what does this have to do with us? I'm glad you asked. Just like a caterpillar, we all as Men have the great potential, latent hidden ability to become the awesome, amazing Man God intends us to be. Also, like a caterpillar we as men can't just sit around and expect it to happen; there are things we must do in order that we might be *Transformed*. Here we go. Just as a caterpillar must eat, we must eat, and I'm not referring to natural food either. Luke 4:4 Jesus says "Man shall not live by bread alone but by every word that proceeds from the mouth of God." I love this because Jesus is speaking of our Spirit man being sustained. Just like we must eat in order to live, and if we don't eat for any significant amount of time we can become malnourished and even die for lack of food. Our Spirit man, in like manner, lives and grows and thrives off of consistently ingesting the word of God. Therefore, if we are going to be transformed as men we must first eat the word of God. It must become more important than anything else in our lives, it must be primary.

The Environment of Accountability

Secondly, like a caterpillar attaches itself to a tree branch, you and I must be connected or attached to a local Church and Pastor. I call this *The environment of accountability*. Remember, no Man is an island unto himself and an unaccountable man is a liability on the battlefield of life. There are so many unaccountable men in the body of Christ today. We must be connected, submitted, and surrendered to something bigger than ourselves. This is absolutely of most importance because it's wrong for a Man to ask his wife to submit and follow him if he is not willing to submit and follow a Leader. A man that has no Pastor is dangerous, we all need accountability. I'll say this quote again, "Isolation will always result in amputation." God made us in such a way that we are to be interdependently connected one to another, so we can resource each other and help each other become truly successful. The Body of Christ is many members, yet we are all individuals. Here's what I mean. My hand is connected to my wrist and my wrist to my arm. My hand is its own part, yet it finds its significance in being connected to my wrist which finds its significance in being connected to my arm. In the same way we are all individuals, but we find our true significance in our submission and connection one to another.

The local Church is extremely important to me; it became an environment for me to glean and emulate other men, I watched how they came to prayer, I watched how they prayed, I watched how they loved their wives and took care of their children. I watched how they opened the car door for their wives and those examples helped to shape my thinking as to what a Man is supposed to be like. I know that not one local church is perfect, but I want to take the time right now to let you know as a Man you need to find a Church with a great Pastor and allow him the place in your heart to help shepherd you and mold you. Get involved in that local Church and watch your wife and children see your example and follow your lead. Years ago, I discovered that the most important decision, second to being born again, was the local church that I would commit to. I discovered that and haven't moved from that mindset. Even though I am currently a Senior Pastor of a Church I am still submitted in every way to my Pastor. Today, Men make decisions based on money, careers, family, and so forth, so many Men have added God to their lives like adding creamer to coffee! We need to make our decisions as men from our solid commitment to the church of the Lord Jesus and our lives will develop out of that decision being primary and not secondary.

Thirdly, as Men if we are going to be transformed and realize our Manhood potential, we need to have a lifestyle of prayer, confession, worship, and meditation of the word of God. I found it to be fascinating that a caterpillar from its own mouth spins its own environment of change. It's amazing that if a caterpillar wouldn't spin its environment, then it would not become the butterfly. Something else pertaining to this is I discovered that one tiny caterpillar can spin a web that is up to three thousand feet in length! What a commitment! The first thing I thought about when I read that was the prayer lives of us as Men. What is our commitment to creating our own environment to become who God called us to be? In the chapter dealing with principles that develop intimacy with God, I discuss how Jesus taught "Men ought always pray and faint not." You and I have been given as Men every necessary tool needed to become the Great Champion of a Man that we are. I'm declaring over you today that you will no longer faint; you will no longer cave in, quit, or turn coward in an area of your life. I declare that as you eat that rich word of God and attach yourself to a local church and get involved in the vision of your pastor, you will through prayer begin to *Spin* your own environment of transformation.

CHAPTER 6

THE ACT OF BECOMING

JOHN 1:12

But as many as received him, to them
gave he power to BECOME the sons of
God, even to them that believe on his name.

Who vs. Do

I love this verse because in a nutshell it's saying that when you and I got born-again as Men we received the right, the privilege, and authority to BECOME who God originally intended us to BE!

The greatest act of a Man is the act of becoming, because once a Man becomes, then and only then does he truly belong. Most men, because of our makeup or the way God designed us, are naturally hunters as I said in the beginning of this book. We are more concerned about accomplishing our goal. You know how we are, we get a target, we aim for it, and then we shoot. Then we run toward our target, pick it up, and raise it up as a trophy because most of us were programmed to find our value in what we accomplish. This is a problem in society now because this mentality, or way of thinking, has caused us to develop Males who have no sense of character. We have raised a generation of men that are more concerned about Results and accomplishment than they are honor and integrity. Again, we want to belong and express our giftedness because we've been taught that acceptance is in the results, so we focus on results regardless of how we got them. We want to BELONG in a marriage, in an occupation, in a certain class of people, in a neighborhood, in a certain economic status, and all these things are important but not the highest priority. This is what I call "Belonging without becoming." Years ago, when The Holy Spirit began to show me the *Blueprint* he gave me a simple quote that has become a brand in my life and ministry and it goes like this, "God is more concerned about your WHO than he is your DO." That's another way of saying "Don't allow your gift to take you to a place where your character can't keep you." Notice without defaming anyone's name that some of the greatest men in our current time and even in history have forfeited their destiny and purpose in life based upon character issues.

God knew this, so just to clearly understand our Heavenly Father's mindset concerning character we can always default back to his first dealings with his first Man in Genesis 1:26, where the scripture says, "and God said, let us make man in our image and after our likeness and let him have dominion." God's first dealing with man teaches us that he sees Character as a high priority, even to the point that he dealt with the man's character before he gave him responsibility. Notice also that he dealt with the man's Character before he gave him a wife! Both of these examples are found in Genesis chapters 1 and 2. I am not saying we should sit around as men and not do anything until we are perfect, that's not at all what I'm saying. What I am saying is that we should not allow what we DO to supersede WHO we are; neither should we allow what we DO to determine WHO we are. Our DO should be the product of our WHO as Men of God.

Jump Right on In

One of the clearest pictures of God prioritizing WHO a man is versus what he does is found in scripture in the book of 1st Samuel 10:5-6, let's look at this story as Men and glean from it.

After that thou shalt come to the hill of God, where is the garrison of the Philistines: and it shall come to pass, when thou art come thither to the city, that thou shalt meet a company of prophets coming down from the high place with a psaltery, and a tabret, and a pipe, and a harp, before them; and they shall prophesy: And the Spirit of the Lord will come upon thee, and thou shalt prophesy with them, and shalt be turned into another man. '

In verse one of 1st Samuel chapter 10 we see Samuel pouring anointing oil over Saul, affirming him as the very first king of Israel. He tells him in verse 1 the Lord Anointed him as captain over his inheritance or people. You would think that would solidify the deal, but Samuel the judge and prophetic voice of that time gives him further instruction that include these fascinating instructions here in verses 5 and 6. Notice that he sends him into an environment where there is a company of prophets who are abruptly playing music and prophetically speaking and declaring and decreeing. This is a shouting Church service here. All the dignified people have left the building! He tells Saul "Now when you get there, jump right in with them and the same spirit that's on them is going to come on you and you are going to start saying, declaring and decreeing just like them" and watch what his last statement is to Saul, "You are going to be *turned* into another Man! The word *turned* here simply means to be converted or to change. Wow! God needed him to deal with his WHO before he focused on his DO. Before he BELONGED as a King he needed to BECOME as a Man! Here is what I'm getting to: if we as Men invest more in BECOMING then when it came to BELONGING in a marriage we would never quit on our wives and family; if we invested in BECOMING then when it came to

BELONGING in an occupation we would never quit! I believe Men are hurting because we bought into the whole DO thing because we wanted to be accepted, and now is the time that we should shift our focus on WHO we are.

The Authentic You

Here is another quote the Lord gave me over the years that helped me on my journey to discovering my personal Significance. *"It's important for YOU to Become YOU, Because Once YOU Become YOU then everything that belongs to you will be attracted to YOU."*

This quote came as a result of meditating scripture. Whenever any individual says they heard from God, then what they believe they've heard must line up with God's written word. In this case I was meditating Genesis chapter 2 and noticed in verse 19 that after God formed the beast of the field and the fowl of the air, he *brought* them unto Adam to see what he would name them. Notice that God *brought* them unto the Man. Again, in chapter 2 verses 21-22 The Lord caused a deep sleep to fall upon Adam and he took one of his ribs and closed the flesh up and made the man a woman and again God *brought* her to the man. This is profound. Notice God dealt with Adam's image (his WHO) in Genesis 1:26, Then what belonged to Adam was *brought* or attracted to Adam (his DO). This speaks volumes when it comes to us as Men. There are Men working dead-end jobs, running from one occupation to the next. Then there are Men in Dead end relationships, running from one female to the next and nothing is working. These verses show God working with the Man, partnering with him. There is no toil involved in these scriptural occurrences. I define toil as T- Trying to O- Operate I- Independent of L- Love. We know God is Love (1st John 4:8), so to *toil* is to attempt to be your own source, independent of God, and *toil* is designed to wear a man out and that is exactly what's happening to so many men. We must understand as John 1:12

says when a man receives Jesus he receives the power to become or come-into-being everything God has planned for him to be, and without Jesus there is no becoming. Once a man becomes, then everything that belongs to him is attracted to him. No toil, man of God: the wife, the assignment, the life God has prepared, you know; the good life. It's all a part of your WHO and not your DO!

What Are YOU Saying About You?

John 1:19-23 And this is the record of John, When the Jews sent priests and Levites from Jerusalem to ask him, who art thou? And he confessed, and denied not; but confessed, I am not the Christ. And they asked him, what then? Art thou Elias? And he saith, I am not. Art thou that prophet? And he answered, no. Then said they unto him, who art thou? That we may give an answer to them that sent us. What sayest thou of thyself? He said, I am the voice of one crying in the wilderness, make straight the way of the Lord, as said the prophet Esaias.

I have the opportunity to meet and mentor so many Men. I believe that this is my Grace! I am here to teach Fatherhood from a biblical perspective and to help make the connection between Fatherhood and Manhood. This is my passion because we have a serious identity crisis today. This crisis starts with the epidemic of fatherlessness and evolves into men not knowing who they are. Then it ends up in our schools and communities and neighborhoods, where children are confused about who they are. They don't understand their gender, and those who have somewhat of an idea of their gender, are just as badly impacted by the fact that they have no idea where they are headed in life. All of this, in my opinion, starts with the Male Man knowing who he is. A Man must know who he is when it comes to manhood because his wife and children are depending on him to know! Again, Our Identity as Men is exclusive to a close, Intimate, personal relationship with God as father through Jesus Christ. I absolutely, unequivocally believe that if we "Change the Men, we can change the world." In my meeting men I get to see so many mindsets. I can pretty much discern them because of my own past experiences, and also the number of Men I have met with or had conversation with. I believe due to so many men growing up in households without a Father around, or having a male figure who did not understand Manhood from a biblical perspective, has caused men to not truly understand who they are. Today there are those who are maturing physically but not experiencing maturation mentally when it comes to being a Man. I think one of the saddest things is to sit and hear a grown Man full of potential and possibility blame everyone else for his lack of success in life. I generally tell those men You can't be pitiful and powerful simultaneously.

In our Men's mentoring program, I get to mentor men from all walks of life. I have noticed that sometimes older gentlemen are more resistant to the teachings of Manhood from a biblical perspective. I believe the reason why has to do with growing up and feeling the need to hang on to belief systems they are accustomed to. Secondly, ego gets in the way and I believe they want to prove their Manhood so much that they resist and refute what could help them. On the other hand almost every young man I mentor with the *Blueprint* system, has grown up, are leaders in the Church, family, and community, Some have even started their own businesses and have become those who are now adding value to our community. These men have become successful in every way. I believe a Man's success in life has everything to do with his understanding of who he is. I have discovered that when a Man knows who he is, he carries himself in a different manner. significant Men don't mind other Men becoming successful; as a matter of a fact they celebrate the success of others. Just recently I posted a picture of Magic Johnson and Dwayne Johnson on social media. This picture was outstanding. The reason why I loved this picture so much is because here were two very successful Men embracing each other and both of them had the most magnetic, genuine smile ever. When I saw that picture I immediately said to myself, here are two individuals that have come into their significance and have capacity to celebrate one another. This is all a product of them knowing and being confident in who they are."

I AM

Here in the book of John we see the Jews sending priests and Levites out to question John of his Identity. I think it's powerful that this text states John confidently knew who he wasn't and who he was. Notice when he was questioned about being the Christ he said, "I AM not the Christ," then they asked him "are you Elias" and he said, "I AM not." Lastly, they said, "are you the prophet" and he said "no." Finally they said this statement and it shook me from the inside out, "who are you? What do YOU SAY of yourself?" Then I can picture John the Baptist in sheer confidence and unwavering candidness say these words," I AM the voice of one crying out in the wilderness making straight the way of the Lord." WOW! I immediately saw from this text that "What YOU say about yourself has everything to do with WHO you are." See it doesn't matter what others say about you, it matters what you say about you. Notice John said "I AM." I heard a profound message by a tremendous general in the body of Christ a few years back and he stated "Whatever follows the words I AM, the universe is wired to see that it comes to pass." You and I as Men must be the prophets of our own lives. I know it's tough sometimes because so many of us have faced terrible circumstances and have had to overcome seemingly insurmountable obstacles. I get that! I also know that what God placed in you must be released in your lifetime, and the battle you face and the tears you may cry to overcome these obstacles in your life will be far less painful than the regret you will experience if you do not realize your full potential as a man.

My Personal Battles

Growing up for me was tough. Trying to get this whole manhood thing together has been my life's journey. Had I not had the encounter I had with God in January of 1991 and the grace he gave me to hunger for his word, I would have been dead long ago. Let me share something with you that I qualify to talk about because I have overcome so much. When I tell a man you can make it, you are great, you are powerful, you will overcome, I am telling him that because I told myself that first. Let me explain. I had to push past my own failures and defeat of life to become who I am today. I appreciate every step of the way. I savor every moment and rejoice in every victory because overcoming, for me, was a real *Faith Fight*. I literally worked the *Blueprint* and am still working it 27 years later. I want to first say I have an awesome mother and she did her absolute best to love and raise me and my siblings. My real father died when I was four years of age and the only real memory I have of him was me being on his shoulders as he walked down Sherwood road in Belleville, Michigan with a bottle of liquor as he gave me a sip in the cold. My step father was a great man who raised 3 children that were not his blood and died at 47 years of age. He was a chronic alcoholic until his death. Our family was torn apart from our childhood. I have two older brothers that I can't remember ever seeing, one of my younger sisters was taken by friends of the family when we were younger, and I didn't see her again until I was 35 years of age. My two siblings and I grew up together and are still a part of each other's lives now. I had my first sexual encounter at around 8 years old with a family member through molestation and after that, consistent encounters of molestation with an uncle until I was almost 15 years of age. These sexual encounters left me sexually addicted were I continued this pattern all through my teenage years with multiple sex partners.

These were just some of the damaging circumstances that made me a young, confused, broken, addicted, sexually confused Man.

I grew angry and self-destructive and became addicted to every kind of drug you can think of. From crack cocaine to weed, powder cocaine, opium ball— you name it! I ran the streets of Detroit and Belleville, Michigan, joined a gang in southwest Detroit, and carried a pistol for almost 2 years of my life. I had no personal value at all. I was in and out of jail as a young man, arrested multiple times. Served probation for years and the only reason I didn't go to prison long term was because the prisons in the 80s were overpopulated. I hurt and injured and damaged others just like I was damaged, because hurting people hurt people. I wasn't waking up wanting to hurt others, but hurt was a part of who I was, and it became my pattern for living.

You Are Your Own Prophet

I said all of this because I wanted you to see that when I tell a Man he can make it, I am speaking from a place of depth! I am speaking from a place of experience and confidence. I had to dig in God's word and say about myself what the word of God said about me, regardless of my current position or mentality of that time. I got up morning after morning confessing and speaking that word. I meditated the word of God so much one family member said to me, "People can go crazy for reading the bible that much." I fell in love with God's word; it was the very first book I ever finished in my life. I began calling myself blessed when I was overcoming the curse. Calling myself whole when my heart was fragmented and broken. I faced every deficit, every inch of Love deficiency, every ounce of fear and failure with the word of God. If I can do it then anyone can! You know they say, "It doesn't matter what others call you, it only matters if you answer to it."

Abram had to call himself Abraham until it manifested, and you can do the same thing in your life Man of God! Get up, be the prophet of your own life. Stand up and say 'I AM who God says I AM.'

I AM Going to the NFL

I remember hearing a story about a young man in our city who went to the NFL. There was a young man who now attends our Church who played football with him in college in Mississippi. He told me that when all the other teammates were done working out at the gym and they were all ready to go and have some social time, this young man would stay in the gym and continue to work out. Some of the other teammates would come to him and say, "Hey man let's go have some fun" and he in turn would say to them, with aggression, "I AM going to the NFL, I AM going to the NFL." Guess what? That young man went to the NFL and his jersey is hanging up in one of our restaurants in our city. See, just like that NFL player, just like John the Baptist, you as a man of God can be the prophet of your own life and overcome every obstacle by saying "I AM," because what YOU say about YOU has everything to do with WHO YOU are.

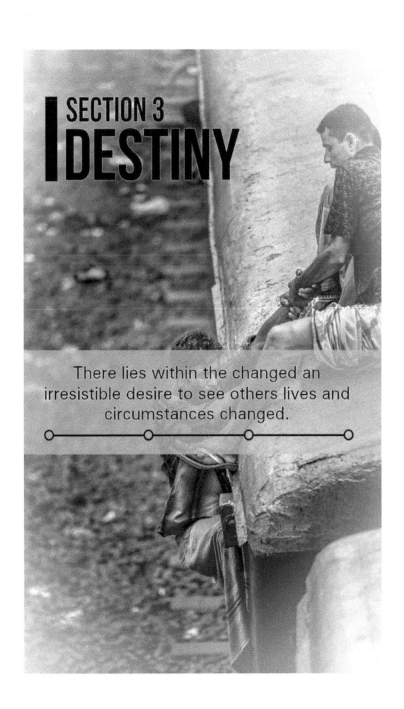

SECTION 3
DESTINY

There lies within the changed an irresistible desire to see others lives and circumstances changed.

CHAPTER 7

HINDRANCES TO DESTINY

LUKE 4:1-4

And Jesus being full of the Holy Ghost returned from Jordan, and was led by the Spirit into the wilderness, being forty days tempted of the devil. And in those days, he did eat nothing: and when they were ended, he afterward hungered. And the devil said unto him, if thou be the son of God, command this stone that it be made bread. And Jesus answered him, saying, it is written, that MAN shall not live by bread alone, but by every word of God.

Putting It All Together

I hope you can now see the Intimacy-Identity connection. This is so important for us as Men to know it's impossible to become who God intended us to be as Men without knowing God as Father intimately. Secondly, in previous chapters we have discussed how WHO we are as Men should be the foundation of what we DO as men. I am so glad our Father created and made us Human BE-ings, not Human DO-ings. A Man's identity in Christ is equal to his Manhood; the two cannot be separated. My aim for the last few chapters is to deal with three important areas pertaining to a Man and his ability to reach his destiny. I am not going to get into detail as to what a Man has been called to do, because I think there are great authors out there that have done a tremendous job in doing that already; I'm more concerned about *The Process* and how it affects a Man's actualization of purpose. The first area we will discuss is *Things that Hinder* or prevent a Man from accomplishing what God has placed him here to do. Secondly, I will show that as a Man we have been wired to *Give Identity* to succeeding generations. This is so important, seeing that so many youths have no concept of who they are and as Men, it's our responsibility to teach them and mentor them so that they may become who God has called them to be and reach their God given potential.

Finally, I will discuss how significance and personal value affect a Man's destiny in life. So, just for the sake of branding this into our thinking, I must revisit the scripture The Holy Spirit gave me years ago that started this whole journey. In John 7:29 again it states, "For I KNOW him (Intimacy), For I AM from him (Identity), He hath sent me (Destiny)." Again, this is what I call the *Blueprint*, and when a Man builds his life according to it, like many others I have discussed in this book, that Man will experience God's best for his life.

The Enemy of Destiny

In the book of Thessalonians chapter 2:18, The Apostle Paul describes, while writing the Church of Thessalonica, his great desire to get to them and to see them. He emphasized that he didn't just try once but twice. He said, "I wanted to come to you but Satan hindered me." I remember thinking to myself when meditating this verse, "How does the enemy have the ability to stop one of the greatest Apostles that ever lived from getting to his desired destination?" Scripture doesn't necessarily say how but it does give us some insight in using the word *Hindered*. I then began to pick this verse apart and discovered the word *Hindered* meant to impede, to detain. One definition I found was to be tedious to, or to cause mental weariness. It's clear the Apostle Paul here had a great desire to see them, yet it's also clear he identified that he was obstructed or hindered by Satan himself! This verse speaks so much to me because it is relevant when it comes to you and I. Like the Apostle Paul, we too have an enemy of our Destiny and our desires. We all have this great desire to accomplish great things, but we need to recognize that the plans God has for us are not without opposition. (Read Ephesians 6:12).

In the book of Luke chapter 4, we also see a great picture of Jesus at the inception of his ministry being tempted and scrutinized by Satan. I believe this temptation was in an effort to delay or to derail his *Destiny*, and just like Jesus, Satan attempts to tempt and entice Men to get them distracted from the great calling and purpose they are here for. He aims to impede, through whatever unchecked or undisciplined area that's in a Man's life, in order to *Hinder* him from getting to his *Destiny*.

The Light of Hope

When dealing with the subject of temptation during our Men's gatherings, this subject is probably the most impacting subject during the Turn Challenge. There is absolutely not one man that is ever present that can't relate to the subject of temptation. What I love about this particular subject is that after going through it, you can see the light of hope turn on in the eyes of men who have been bound and addicted. These are men who have great dreams and great desires they would like to accomplish in life, but struggle with issues like every one of us. Most of these Men come to the program thinking there was no hope for them at all. I use this scripture in Luke chapter 4 as our foundation because we see that even the Lord Jesus himself had to overcome temptation while living in a physical body during his earthly ministry. The word tempted here means the enemy tested or scrutinized Jesus. Another meaning is to entice or to examine. The enemy was looking for some door of access into his life. Notice the question the devil kept bringing before the Lord was, *"If thou be the Son of God."* I think it's fair here to say that this temptation was a test to get Jesus to act outside of WHO he was. I call this particular group of verses, *The Identity Test,* and just like Jesus every man will face his Identity test because the enemy is after a Man's effectiveness in the earth.

I always say God never creates anything or anyone without purpose and Destiny. The devil knows that, and because he knows that he is sending everything he has against Men in this generation. He knows that as goes the Man, so goes the marriage and as goes the marriage, so goes the family, and as goes the family, so goes the Church, the community, the city, the nation, the world. Again, it all starts with the Male Man! Here Jesus is at the beginning of his ministry and knowing who he was had everything to do with his ability to fulfill his earthly assignment. Jesus painted a picture for every man here how to overcome temptation, and I love how the Holy Spirit wanted to show us that Jesus overcame temptation through his absolute dependency upon the written word of God.

One of the key things I want to point out is that the devil knew the capacity of the Son of God. He told Jesus, "If you are the Son of God, command that these stones be made bread." Satan knew how to locate the son of God; he knew the potential and the power the son of God would walk in. Just like he knew the capacity of Jesus, He knows your purpose, he knows your potential and he's looking for an entry point into our lives as Men, because the devil knows if he can shut the Man down he can shut the family down, and the family is the cornerstone of society from which we build.

He Has Nothing IN Me

One of my most favorite scriptures in the bible is found in the book of John 14:30. Jesus has been teaching his disciples and he says something very powerful, "Hereafter I will not talk much with you: for the prince of this world cometh, and hath *nothing in me!"* Glory to God. That's where we must be as Men, in a place that the enemy can't find anything in us! A place where he has absolutely no entry point.

Let me explain what an entry point is. In the financial realm, an entry point is when the seller *lowers* the standard price in order for the buyer to be on agreeable terms. That means there is *no entry point* when the standard is too high for the buyer. Wow! That's what I mean, as Men our standard must be too high for Satan to gain entry. When the standard is high there are no agreeable terms. See, that's what happened with Jesus. His standard was too high for Satan to gain entry in his life; that's why he told his disciples in John 14:30, "He hath nothing in me."

If you were to look at Matthew's rendition in (Chapter 4:9 ASV) the enemy said to Jesus, "all these things will I give thee, if thou will fall down and worship me." This is powerful! Satan was letting us know that Jesus had to fall or lower his standard in order for him to use him. Earlier I mentioned in the book that when Adam fell, he didn't fall geographically, He fell in his thinking. He quit thinking like his heavenly Father and started thinking like a mere Man without divine assistance. Here is another thing we need to know about this text. When he requested that Jesus fall down and worship, he wasn't talking about just simply bowing or singing a song. Worship is a lifestyle. Satan here was requesting that Jesus fall from thinking and *living* like a Son of God, and then live like a mere man. That's the only way he could use him. Notice that Jesus countered his request with the word of God, because the only way to walk in this kind of victory over temptation is to walk in the word. Every jab that the enemy threw at Jesus, he retaliated with the written Word of God. Also notice that in verse 1 the scripture teaches that Jesus was *full* of the Holy Spirit and as a result he was *led* by the Holy Spirit. This is powerful for us as men as we charge toward our Destiny in life; we must be *full* in order that we may be *led*. Now the Holy Spirit only leads and guides by the written word of God (See John 16:13), so we must keep that in mind. I tell men that in life, we will always have battles with sin, our flesh, and the devil, and the primary weapon we have to overcome with is the written word of

God. This is the exact weapon that Jesus used in overcoming the scrutinizing of the enemy.

Sexual Temptation

I think it's very important that we as men deal with certain issues that may seem uncomfortable. One of the issues we must face and overcome is the area of sexual temptation. It has been one of the most used tools by the enemy to cause many great Men to forfeit or fail when it comes to fulfilling their *Destiny*. Statistics state that forty million Americans are regular visitors to porn sites. They say that seventy percent of Men between the ages of eighteen to twenty-four visit porn sites in a typical month. Twenty percent of men admit to watching porn and Men are six times more likely to watch porn than women. The part that hit me was that statistics say that fifty percent of religious men are addicted to pornography, so this problem is not just an issue outside of the church, but it has become a major issue within the church. I personally believe that every Man has dealt with some type of sexual temptation. Literally every man I know has had to fight the temptation to overcome sexual sin. Why is this important that we face it? We have seen some of the greatest political figures, CEO's of major companies, pastors, and even families being dismantled and shredded to pieces due to infidelity in the lives of men. Now I'm not saying that only men battle in this area but what I am saying is that we must recognize that there is a problem and face it head on, so we can overcome the hindrances of the enemy of our Destiny and realize our god given potential as men.

(Source: stats on men and pornography. Pornography addiction among men is on the rise/HuffPost.)

Nothing New Under the Sun

I was asked a question in an interview on a Christian television network on one of the main hindrances for men when fulfilling their potential. They wanted to know what some of the things are that stop great men from succeeding. My answer was this, *vices*. They asked what does that mean? I began to talk to them about *vice* grips, a certain tool that you can lock on an object and it would be extremely difficult to get the grip off. I then began to teach them what God gave to me as an acronym for the word VICE. Vicious Impulse that Cripples a person's Effectiveness. Every one of us as Men wants to be effective, to be effective means to be successful in producing a desired or intended result. We all want results as men, don't we? I don't necessary believe that it's the desire that stops us; I believe it's the distractions that we don't overcome through faith that hinder us. It's the *Vicious Impulses* that hinder most men from becoming great.

A *Vicious* impulse is an immoral, merciless, strong urge or desire that controls a man and prevents him from fulfilling his potential. We see this is the book of Judges Chapters 13-16 in the life of Samson who has this incredible anointing and destiny on his life, but he also has a *vice* in the form of Delilah. You know the story, she entices him, discovers the source of his power (His Hair or Nazarite vow), cuts his hair, and he becomes a victim to the Philistines. Notice that when you read the story, the first thing they do after taking him captive is to gouge out his eyes, they take his vision. This is powerful because where there is no vision the people perish (Proverbs 29:18).

Another story is about Esau, the elder twin brother of Jacob. In Genesis 25:29-34, Esau returns from the fields thirsty and faint. He asks his brother Jacob, who is making a pot of stew, to give him some. Jacob in turn swindles Esau out of his birthright. Now in looking at this event most would say "Look at Jacob, he's a trickster and a schemer," and they would be absolutely correct in saying that. But the real problem wasn't with Jacob, it was with Esau. When you read verse 32 the bible says that Esau said, "Behold, I am at the point to die: and what profit shall this birthright do to me?" This is amazing here because when you see it for what it is; you see that Esau did not understand his personal value! He did not know his worth. He allowed a temporary satisfaction to superimpose the Blessing of his birthright. He lowered his standard, or his image of himself, creating an *Entry Point* that gave access for him to forfeit his *Destiny*. Now don't go saying "I would never do that." Many Men have forfeited their *Destiny* for a little money, a night with a female outside of their marriage, a little alcohol, or maybe just a little compromise.

Here is something else that the Lord showed me about temptation. Often, we think that we have to pray that the bar is shut down, or we have to pray that the casino is shut down, and we have to pray that the strip club is shutdown, or we pray against the pornography industry to shut down. As Christians we get our prayer groups together and point at locations like these and command them to shut down, but the problem is not the locations that I mentioned. Just like Jacob wasn't Esau's problem, Jacob only revealed what was already in Esau; the strip club only reveals what was already in the man who went in. The casino only reveals what was already in the gambler. If those things are in a man, then wherever he goes he will find them! "Wherever YOU are, YOU are." Proverbs 23:7 tells us that "as a Man thinks in his heart, so is he." As men we must fight for our *Destiny*, we must fight for our marriages, we must fight for our children and our children's children! There are multiple stories that we could discuss such as David and Bathsheba, Solomon and his hundreds of concubines. These are all examples of Men who allow temptation to cost them *Destiny*." We as Men must allow the word to cleanse and purify our hearts so like Jesus we can truly say, "He Hath NOTHING IN me."

Overcoming Temptation

Now that we have discussed temptation and vicious impulses that cripple a man's effectiveness, let's talk about overcoming them. As I said at the beginning of this chapter, Jesus painted a clear picture to every man how we are to overcome temptation. I mentioned that Jesus fought temptation with the written word of God, and just like he used the word, a man must master using the word to overcome. If you'll read Luke 4:1-13 and see this event where Jesus is being examined and scrutinized by the devil, Jesus answers every attack with the written word spoken out of his mouth. The Apostle Paul calls this, in Ephesians chapter 6:17-18 when teaching the Church of Ephesus about this spiritual battle, the sword of the Spirit. The amplified bible says that it's "the sword that the spirit wields which is the word of God." Listen, every word of God has enough power within itself to bring itself to pass, but God's word has no power until you and I take it off the pages, put it in our mouths, and declare it by faith! That's exactly what Jesus did, he declared it over and over and over until finally verse 13 in Luke chapter 4 says, "And when the devil had ended all the *temptation*, he departed from him for a season." I like to say the devil "Tucked tail and ran like a dog." If speaking the word worked for Jesus as a Man when he was being tempted, then speaking the word will work for you and I.

In conclusion to this chapter, James 4:7 says, "Submit yourselves therefore unto God, resist the devil and he will flee." There is no submission to God without submitting to his word, God and his word are inseparable. He and his word are one and the same. When God speaks a thing, he then commits himself to the fulfillment of what he has spoken. When we submit ourselves to his word we are submitting ourselves to God, this then enables us to resist the devil. The word *resist* means to stand against and to oppose, but when a Man has a weak human spirit, it's difficult for him to resist any form of temptation. Picture temptation as weights in a gym. When a Man consistently goes to the gym and works out, his ability to *resist* the weight gets better day by day because he's getting stronger. In like manner, the more we ingest or consume the word of God regularly, the more our human Spirit gets stronger and stronger and that enables us to resist temptation.   Proverbs 18:14 MSG says, "A healthy Spirit conquers adversity." This means when we have a strong spirit or inner man, we can resist the enemy of our Destiny. If you understand that just like your physical body grows and develops based upon what you put in it, then you can fully understand that you are a Spirit and you need to eat the word of God, so that you can grow and develop into a strong individual that can be used by God to advance the Kingdom of God. We can see this spiritual development and strength in the life of Jesus as a child. The book of Luke chapter 2:40 says, "And the child grew, and waxed strong in spirit, filled with wisdom: and the grace of God was upon him." This is what happens when a Man builds his inner man up by feeding on the word of God— he grows and waxes strong in spirit. Here the words wax strong means that he was empowered by the Holy Spirit, he increased in vigor or became powerful and mighty. Just like Jesus, every Man can be empowered by the Holy Spirit as he builds himself up in God's word and then, as the book of James says we are enabled to, "Resist the devil and he will flee!"

CHAPTER 8

THE AUTHORITY TO GIVE IDENTITY

GENESIS 2:19

"and out of the ground the lord God formed every beast of the field, and every fowl of the air; and brought them unto Adam to see what he would call them: and WHATEVER Adam, CALLED every living creature, that was the NAME thereof.

A Sparked Interest

I was a young bible student at my local church, taking laymen's bible classes so that I could eventually become a minister of the gospel. We were on the subject of patriarchs of faith and how that a number of Men that God used, their names were changed. It intrigued me to know that Abram became Abraham and Jacob became Israel, Simon became Peter and Saul became Paul. This interest sparked another interest in me, and that was to find out what my name meant. At the time I was about 25 years old. I was hungry to know my purpose and destiny. I wanted to accomplish great things and felt that after having learned somewhat about these bible characters and how their encounters with God changed their names, I then really needed clarity about my name. At that particular time, we didn't have Google or Siri, so I couldn't just push the button on my iPhone and ask Siri. Secondly, I was so poor and impoverished minded then that I couldn't even afford a computer to try and look it up so, I went and bought a small book for picking out names for children and was happy to see my name in the book. I found out my name Claude meant: weak, crippled, lame, impotent. I couldn't believe it, but no matter how many times that I read it, it never changed. I remember being furious. I began thinking, "What was wrong with my parents when they named me this?" I could only remember that the instructor of the bible class was saying that Jacob was a "trickster and a Schemer' and how he mentioned that that's what his name meant. Those words were running through my head, and for some reason, having not studied Hebrew culture at the time, I somehow knew that a person's name determined their *Identity* and their *Identity* determined their *destiny.* I began to be depressed, I felt like God had no purpose and plan for me. To make it worse, every time someone called me, "Claude," It was as if the weakness, impotence, lameness would just grow more solid in my thinking. I felt that I was destined for failure. It literally affected every area of my life. I began to tell everyone, and no matter who I told, it deemed no one could fix it. I even went as far as going to my mother and asking her did she know what my Father's name meant because I was named after him. This negative mindset continued in me until one of my mentors found another definition of my name and it was this, "The fragile one, easily broken by God." To this day I still don't know where he got that definition from, but all I know is that I was thankful that he did. Somehow this new definition liberated my thinking, and it felt like the weight of the world was lifted completely from me. I'm not saying that I stopped thinking about my names definition right at that moment, but the healing process began in my life from that point.

I'm Seeing It Everywhere

This whole name thing was branded in my thinking by now; it was as if God allowed it so that I would give my attention to it because by this time, I was seeing this whole name changing thing from a completely different perspective. I learned years ago that if you want to understand the end of a thing then you must go back to the beginning; you must locate it at its inception and discover God's original intention at its origin. I began looking at the creation account in Genesis chapter 1 and noticed that God created everything by speaking it into existence. He commanded light to be and it was, he then separated light from darkness, and then he *Called* light day and darkness night. Then he created a firmament and divided the waters from the waters, and dry land appeared, then he *Called* the dry land Earth and the gathering together of the waters he *Called* them Seas. When you look at the first chapter of Genesis, you see God creating and then *Calling* everything, but the *Calling* stops at verse 10. After verse 10 he creates every living thing from vegetation to beast of the field, great creatures of the sea to fowl of the air, then he makes a Man in his own image and likeness and gives him the complete authority to rule and govern the earth and everything he created. Then I saw something so profound that it shook the core of my very being. I remember reading Genesis 2:19 and seeing God bringing animals and all creation unto Adam, and I noticed something that caused me to leap out of my seat: God stopped *Calling* and now you see he gives that responsibility to the Man. The verse reads like this: "Whatever Adam called them, that was the name thereof." I began to look up the word *Called* and discovered that it meant to *Address by Name* and when you named something or someone, according to Hebrew culture you are giving it or them their Identity. This means that God as father gave his son Adam *The Authority to give Identity*. I was so empowered to see this, so I began to study more, and it was everywhere. In Genesis 2:22-23 we see God placing Adam in a deep sleep, he then takes the rib of the man and creates a WOMBman or a man with a womb, then repeats the process that he did with every other living thing by bringing her unto Adam to see what he would name her, and Adam then gave Identity to his wife. I saw two very important things in this account of scripture; the first was that God as Father, out of his significance made the man *just like himself* and allowed the Man to share in the creative process by giving him responsibility to give identity to everything created.

Secondly, I saw the vast importance of a Man and his relationship with God as Father being the source of the Man's ability to be creative and give identity. Here's what I mean: if a Man breaks fellowship with God as Father, then the man loses his significance and personal value, this is what happened to Adam when he left the presence of God. A Man who is absent from an intimate relationship with his heavenly Father will *Call* or name people, places and things improperly! Now you and I can realize how important it is for a Man to have his life in order pertaining to his fellowship with God, because based upon his intimate walk with God would determine his ability to give Identity. I'm going to deal with last at the close of this chapter.

Back to Abraham

The most interesting picture of this played out, to me, was in the life of Abram and Sarai. I mentioned earlier that Abram and his ability to see the manifestation of the promise that God gave him was not due to the sovereign timing of God! God is eternal, he's outside of time. It's our faith in the covenant that causes manifestation of whatever God has promised us to come to pass. As I said previously it was Abram's self-perception that was hindering the manifestation of what God promised. Again, in Genesis 17: verses 1-16 we see all of this play out. Verse 1, Abram gets a revelation of God as "The almighty, impregnable God who is capable of conceiving." Once he *sees* God in this fashion he then in turn is able to *see* himself differently. God tells Abram in verse 5 to Stop *Calling* or naming yourself

Abram because that is not How I *see* you! Abram, you must *see* yourself as ABRAHAM! Now start *Calling* yourself "Abraham". This personal Intimacy with God Changed Abram's Identity to Abraham. God revealed Abrams significance as Abraham in that place of intimacy, glory to God. Now finally, God gets to the final issue, he says, "Abraham, now that you know who you are, now that you are significant stop *Calling* your wife Sarai because that means dominant woman. Out of your significance start *Calling* her Sarah because that means, Lady and princess, and when you do this, I will Bless her. Now if you remember Genesis 2:19 it says that "Whatever the Man *named* every living creature, that was the name thereof." This is so profound because if you notice, we are the ones giving Identity to everything and everyone around us. We are naming sicknesses, diseases, and the conditions of this world. God's not *Calling* these things, we are! God can't get into this earth to give identity except he does it through a Man. Man still has dominion, he is still in authority. He is either sourced by God or sourced by Satan. We really need to get this in us as Christian Men, because while we are sitting back waiting for Jesus to return and rapture us out of this "Terrible God forsaken planet," God is attempting to get some Man, any Man, to *see* things as he *sees* them, he's attempting to turn some "Abrams into Abrahams" so his kingdom can be advanced in the earth. Adam gave Identity to everything including his wife, Abraham gave Identity to Sarah, and all throughout scripture you will see that Man has been given *the authority to give identity*. I want to take time to reiterate right here that Abram kept *Calling* his wife Sarai. His perception of his wife was a projection of himself! When a Man doesn't know or *sees* his significance and personal value, he can't *see* it in his wife, his children, or anyone for that matter. Insignificant Men can't *see* greatness in anyone else; their own low self-esteem won't allow them to! Therefore, we must solidify that Manhood is something that can only be actualized through a close intimate personal relationship with God as father through Jesus Christ. We are always going to view people, places, and things based upon our own self-image. That's why the whole story starts with a Father giving identity to his Son (Genesis 1:26).

From a Bar to a Blessing

In the western hemisphere, we have a problem with giving some of the strangest names. I believe it's due to the fact that we've never been taught the importance of names and how that *naming* someone is a picture of their Identity and a person's Identity determines their destiny. When my wife and I first started our local church almost 10 years ago, we were reaching out to some of the most neglected youth in our city. We had a 2001 white Dodge van, it was already used when we purchased it, but we put so much wear and tear on it that the transmission gave out. We drove all over our small city of Adrian, Michigan, picking up all the fatherless kids from broken homes. We had a burden to reach them because every time my wife and I would see them our hearts would sink. We both remembered growing up in similar conditions like them. Our tiny church began to take root within the city, and boy was I not even ready for what was about to happen next. We began to experience attacks from every angle. The property we were in was a bar that was connected to a hotel, and we were in an agreement to pay 1,900.00 per month for a five thousand square foot facility. We had no money at all, it was pure faith for us to make the arrangement, and to make it worse our congregation was a bunch of children and teens. The only adults that we had were about 4 of us, that included myself, my wife, another Gospel rapper that helped me start the church, and his fiancé who soon became his wife. However, we didn't care because I had a word from God. I had meditated John chapter 4:36 where Jesus was teaching about the harvest of souls and how those who would reap the harvest would get the wages. I ran with it like this, "If I get the people, then God would write the paycheck." I knew that I was deployed by God and he was our only source. The more we began to reach the youth, the more attacks would come. The hotel went into foreclosure without us knowing, we stayed there with no electricity and we had prayer vigils with candles for real, because we had to! Thank God it was summer because we didn't need gas. The city helped us transfer the water into our name, so we could keep it on. This went on for a while until we were eventually able to get the electricity turned on, but not the traditional way. During that stage of the ministry we had a Messianic Jewish gentleman who joined the church, and he knew how to wire electrical from generators to the circuit box. It was amazing! We started those two generators up and the power in the building came on. Needless to say I was excited; "Halleluiah, no more candlelight services." Eventually after that, the hotel started up a new brand and renegotiated a new contract with us. Now we have real lights, gas, and water on in the building and we are reaching 50 kids or so, and the city comes in and gives us a city eviction based upon a newspaper article about our church taking over the bar section of the hotel. They said we weren't zoned properly. On top of that we were experiencing backlash from some parents because all the kids called me and my wife "Dad and Mom." During this time of ministry, we began to reach a lot of young girls that were confused about their identity. Some were thinking they were lesbian and I was attempting to be a solid Father figure to them and teach them who they were in Christ, and of course giving them God's word on the matter. However, the epidemic of lesbianism continued to grow and the attacks on my wife and I grew also. Then one day in sheer desperation I cried out to God and asked him, "Why is this so hard? What's up with all these attacks against what we are doing, did I miss you?" The pressure was so overwhelming that we both just wanted to quit. By that time, I had slowed down doing any Gospel rap and became more focused on the church and all the youth we were reaching. Also, more adults had come but not enough to pay the bills consistently. My desperation grew, and God responded to my desperate cry, He placed it on my heart to do research on the name of our city. He told me "I would find the problem within the name."

As I began to look on the internet and discover the origin of the name Adrian, I noticed that it was supposed to be named the village of Logan, but the wife of the Man who founded the city was fascinated by a roman emperor named Hadrian. What was even more interesting is that there were four areas that I call strongholds that this person, that our city was named after experienced. He was a pedophile; he also caused persecution to the church of his time. He was in a homosexual relationship and had suicidal tendencies until his death. In our city we were experiencing all of these strongholds. It was like the light turned on, and I was then armed with what I needed to do. Since then my wife and I have grown the church to over 200 faithful people, and that's massive coming from a small rural city surrounded by cornfields with a population of 20,000 people, and I am an African American Pastor with a Caucasian wife. Almost all of those teenagers have been delivered from addictions, lesbianism, drugs, and violence. Most of them have grown up, got married, started families, and are leaders now in our church. All these things changed for a number of reasons, but one of the first reasons is that once I identified the problem in the name, I changed the name spiritually to *The City of Eden*. We began to develop prayer confessions and call the city "Eden, Michigan," One time I got very bold, during a shooting in our city the mayor came out to a local park where I gathered Men to do a prayer walk with me to stop the violence, and I mentioned to the mayor that we needed to change the name of the City: he laughed but I was very serious. Some would say, Pastor Claude, it doesn't take all that. My response is that everything you and I see was created by words. Words determine the outcome of our lives, Proverbs chapter 18:21 says that "Death and life are in the power of the tongue," so when we use words to name something or someone, we are determining their outcome. I gained insight through the word of God pertaining to this from a story in the scriptures about Jacob and his wife Rachel.

The Man and His Authority

In the book of Genesis chapter 35:16-18 we see Rachel the wife of Jacob giving birth to a son, the scripture calls it "Hard Labor." This was a time of tremendous pain and agony for Rachel. It became so intense that verse 18 says that *"It came to pass, as her soul was departing, (For she died) that she called his name Benoni: but his FATHER Called him Benjamin."* Rachel, in her pain and sorrow *named* her son according to her experience. The word Benoni actually means *The son of my sorrow,* but Jacob his Father stepped up and *called* him Benjamin, which means *Son of my right hand.* This story is a picture of not only the authority a Man has been given, but also the awesome responsibility that he has been given. I'm not by any means implying that women don't have authority in the body of Christ, if it weren't for women in the church, most churches wouldn't survive. There are accounts of great women throughout the entire bible who have revolutionized our world for the good, but this book isn't about womanhood, it's about Manhood. What I am attempting to do is to herald a gospel to Men from every walk of life, empowering them with Fatherhood and Manhood from a biblical perspective. My aim is to show that only the Male Man has been given authority to give Identity. There is so much to say about this. We live in a time where feminism is at an all-time high; our children have been inundated with error pertaining to the family structure. This confusion has led our youth to a place of utter Identity crisis. As I mentioned in the beginning of the book, they are experiencing fear, poverty, lack of Identity— including both homosexuality and lesbianism— school shootings, transgenderism, teenage pregnancy, sexually transmitted diseases, abortion, incarceration, and much more. All these things that they are facing are the product of the lack of order in our families, and we must begin to see and build our families from a biblical perspective if we are going to see God's purpose and plan played out in our lives. We as Men must stand up and take our rightful place in our marriages, families, churches, communities and so forth. I love this story because this is not the beginning of Jacob's experience, this is the result of his experience. This is the product of a journey of a Man who was transformed in the presence of God. I believe that this picture is a lot more aggressive than we think. Let me explain. Jacob was a Man who was in search of his significance and personal value. He was loved by his mother and scripture seems to show that his father Isaac may have favored Esau. Esau seemed to be a hunter, a man's man, but Esau did not value his birthright and Jacob swindled him out of it. Jacob, though he was a trickster and schemer was a Man that was looking to discover himself. In Genesis 32 (read whole chapter) we find Jacob leaving his uncle Laban's after working for him for 21 years, now ready to come into his own. Jacob was confused and still in fear of the repercussions of his former dealings with his elder brother Esau. During this needed time of his self-discovery journey, Jacob finds what I call again *The Blueprint*. In Genesis 32:7 we see Jacob afraid and greatly distressed about his brother's coming to meet him. He then begins to devise a plan in fear of Esau. He separated his flocks and herds into two bands, still being deceptive and self-aware, looking to save himself. In Genesis 32:9 Jacob cries out to God, he placed his dependency completely upon God. This is the first step of the *Blueprint*. He begins to confess the promises before God that were made to him. After Jacob ran out of all his scheming he sent his wives, women servants, and eleven sons over the brook and sent everything he had with them. Then verse 24 says that "Jacob was left alone" and there wrestled a Man with him until the breaking of the day. Verse 25 says "and when he saw that he prevailed not against him, he touched the hollow of his thigh; and the hollow of Jacob's thigh was out of joint, as he wrestled with him." Here is the point. During this time of wrestling (Intimacy), Jacob would not let him go, Verse 26 says, "I will not let you go until you bless me," Then verse 27 brings it home, "And he said unto him, what is your name?" Now, if you don't look deeply into this you might miss it. When he asked him what his name was, The Hebrew defines the word "name" as character. This intimate wrestling match was to deal with Jacob's perception of himself. Wow! God was going after the source of Jacobs' deceptive, cunning and trickery mindset, he went to the root of his problem and that was the way he saw himself. Just like Jacob, every Man's character or Image or self-perception or how he sees himself will determine his effectiveness in life. Jacob's problem wasn't Esau, nor was it his uncle Laban, nor was it his mother or Father. Jacob's problem was how he saw himself. Notice that Jacob's response to the man was "My name is Jacob," You know me, I am who everyone says that I am, I am a trickster, a schemer, a deceiver. I looked up one other meaning of his name and it meant: "The last." He was saying, I am the last to get the wife, the last to get the job, the last to get the raise, the last to overcome, the last to be successful, I am the Last. Can't you see it? This image he had of himself was a pitiful self-sabotaging perception of himself. God, or any individual in the universe cannot help a Man that sabotages his own destiny by the way he perceives himself.

From Being Changed to Changing His Son's Identity

Now my favorite part is when the man tells him during this time of wrestling (Intimacy) in verse 28," Thy name shall be *called* no more Jacob, but Israel: for as a prince hast thou power with God and with men and has prevailed." After this encounter Jacob recognizes that this was a God encounter; in verse 30 it says, *"And Jacob called the name of that place Penial: for I have saw God face to face, and my life is preserved."* No matter how you look at this story, we see Jacob having an Intimate encounter with God. This Intimate encounter causes him to change his name (Identity), his self-perception. Jacob said it himself, "When I seen God face to face, I was changed." That's the plan that God has for every Man is a face to face encounter that transforms our lives so we as Men can transform this world. Now let's look at how these two stories connect. I first needed to take you to this part of

Jacob's life so that you would both understand and value the part of his life when he rises as a Father and gives Identity to his son. I believe that Jacob understood that names meant something, and that they would determine a person's Identity and destiny. I believe that the struggle that Jacob went through, discovering and realizing his significance, was the fuel for him to intervene in this matter. I can picture him completely overriding the identity of sorrow and pain given to his son by his mother. I believe he knew that the *name* that she gave him would bring to him sorrow and pain. As a result, Jacob as a Father named his son, giving him a name that would bring great significance; Benjamin, instead of having a destiny of pain and sorrow, his father gave him a destiny of power! This is the authority that we as Men and Fathers have and must walk in. Just like Jacob we have been given the right, *just because we are Men,* to give Identity to everyone and everything around us. Listen, if you don't believe this let me help you. The presence of a Man, the presence of a Father makes a major difference in society. The Department of Health and Human Services completed a study in 1996 and some of the statistics are as follows:

1. Only 1 in 4 children live now with their paternal Fathers.

2. 42% of female-headed households with children were poor, compared to 8% of children with both parents.

3. Girls without Fathers in their lives are 2 and ½ times more likely to get pregnant and 53% more likely to commit suicide.

4. Boys without Fathers in their lives are 63% more likely to run away from home and 37% more likely to use drugs.

5. Boys and girls without a Father's involvement are twice as likely to drop out of school, twice

as likely to go to jail and nearly four times more likely to need help for emotional and behavioral problems. This is very important due to our recent rash of school shootings. 26 of 27 of the young Men that committed these acts of indiscretion were all "Fatherless." *Source (realclearpolitics.com)*

6. The average American Father spends only 7 ½ uninterrupted minutes per week with his children but 32 hours a week watching TV.

7. 85.5% of America's 1.1 million annual abortions occur among unmarried women. Source *(lifenews.com-Dadsmatter:)*

These are just a few of the statistics that prove that Fatherhood, Manhood presence is extremely necessary in the lives of children. The absence of Male presence and his giving of identity has brought about these circumstances. If we don't address Manhood from a Biblical perspective then this slope of destruction of marriage, family, church, community, and society will continue to get worse. I read some other material that stated if a Father doesn't go to church, no matter how faithful his wife's devotions are, only one child in 50 will become a regular worshipper. If a Father does go, but irregularly to Church, regardless of his wife's devotion, between a half and two thirds of their offspring will find themselves coming to church regularly or occasionally. A non-practicing mother with a regularly-attending Father will see a minimum of two-thirds of her children ending up in Church. In contrast, a non-practicing Father with a regular mother will see two thirds of his children never darken the door of the church, and if his wife is similarly negligent that figure rises to 80%. Fatherhood and Manhood presence is extremely important to our society!

One day, I was at a Christian television network in Detroit Michigan doing a program called *Ask the Pastor*. The atmosphere was already set and filled with God's presence due to the very successful show that we just completed. I began talking with a seasoned pastor, a very anointed Man of God whom I love and genuinely look up to. He is a true asset to the body of Christ. He began to speak to me, sharing with me that he had admired my desire to see Men step up and take their place. I began to converse with him about my vision for restoring the hearts of the fathers back to the children and the hearts of the children back to the Fathers, in order to bridge the gap between generations. During my conversation I began to express some of my concerns with Fatherhood and Manhood in general, but he quickly corrected me with such love and accuracy by saying, "Pastor Bevier, the very fact that they are Males means that they have *potential* to be *Men* and the very fact that they are *Men* means that they have it within them to be Fathers." That correction that he so lovingly gave me was so smooth that I didn't recognize it until I had left and was more than five miles down the road. When it hit me, I immediately called him and thanked him for lovingly correcting me. This encouragement from my good friend to me is an encouragement to all Men that regardless of the current state any Man may be in, the very fact that we are Male means that we have Manhood and Fatherhood potential.

The Words of a Father

Luke 1:19-20 And the angel answering said unto him, I am Gabriel, that stand in the presence of God; and am sent to speak unto thee, and to shew thee these glad tidings. 20 And, behold, thou shalt be dumb, and not able to speak, until the day that these things shall be performed, because thou believest not my words, which shall be fulfilled in their season.

Growing up as a child, we would all play games. It doesn't matter what background you may have come from, we all played games.

We played hide and seek, tag, football, basketball, and many more. One thing that seemed to always occur during the fun is one of us would get upset or mad at the other because we lost the game or got hurt, and then we would start the name calling. We would say hurtful things to each other. I remember an old saying that we all seemed to have memorized, it went like this: "Sticks and stones may break my bones, but names will never hurt me." Everybody knew that saying and everyone used that saying without fully understanding it. The truth is, sticks and stones can break your bones, but Names can destroy your destiny. In Luke chapter 1 verses 5-25, we find a very important story about a Man by the name of Zacharias. This story reveals a few very important things to you and I as Men; first it clearly shows the authority that we as Men have. Secondly, it teaches the great responsibility a Man has to cooperate with God in the giving of identity to the next generation, and thirdly it paints how important the identity-destiny connection is in all of our lives.

Zacharias was a priest of the course of Abias and was married to a woman named Elizabeth, the first cousin of Mary who became the mother of Jesus. He was fulfilling his priestly orders, after his custom. The scripture says that both the Man and his wife were righteous and walked in all the commandments and ordinances of the Lord, but one thing was missing in their lives; they had no child due to Elizabeth being barren. As Zacharias was fulfilling his priestly duties within the temple burning incense, the whole multitude of people were praying at the time of the incense. Then the angel of the Lord appeared to Zacharias and said, "don't fear, your prayers are heard, and your wife Elizabeth is going to have a son and you Zacharias are going to call him John." Then the angel began to reveal to him all the great things that would be a part of John's destiny and how he would be the forerunner to the ministry of the Lord Jesus. He mentioned how he would bring joy and gladness to Zacharias, how he would be full of the Holy Ghost even from his mother's womb, and how he would function in the Spirit and power of Elisha. Then, after all that powerful angelic encouragement, Zacharias opened his mouth and said, "How is all this going to happen? I am old, and my wife is well stricken in years...." Wow! I hope you can see this. Look at how Zacharias *sees* himself, and notice that how he *sees* himself, he then projects that on his wife. Immediately following these words released out of Zacharias mouth, the angel responded without flinching and without apology. In verse 19 He said, "*I am Gabriel, that stand in the presence of God; I have been sent to speak unto you, and to show you these glad tidings. And, behold, you shall be dumb, and not able to SPEAK, until the day that these things shall be performed, because you don't believe my words, which shall be fulfilled in their season.*" This is a mouth full here so let's see what happened, so we can learn from this example. Zacharias' poor self-image of himself was causing him to project the same thing on his wife. He said, "I am old, and my wife is well stricken in age." The story shows us that he must have been praying for a child because the angel told him that his prayers were heard. It is clear that Zacharias as the Father of John the Baptist could have, through his own insignificance, projected his unbelieving image on his wife Elizabeth and she could have never conceived the child (verse 24). Also, I believe that the words of a Father are so potent that the angel Gabriel had to shut Zacharias mouth because his unbelieving, poor perception of himself would have cost the destiny of John the Baptist! In my opinion His wife is full of faith. She seems like one of us. This may sound humorous, but I heard those first five months of pregnancy are the most important. Those are the months where you need to watch what you eat; watch everything that you do because that little baby is in there being formed and taking shape. The bible says that when she conceived, she hid! I think Elizabeth was standing in faith believing, praying and when she conceived she said, "I'm getting away from anything and anyone that could cause me to lose this baby." The story goes on where Elizabeth finally has the baby and all the family and friends are around and Zacharias is still mute and unable to speak because of his unbelief. On the 8th day they are circumcising the baby and called him Zacharias after his Father's name and Elizabeth steps up and says "No, his name is John." The family and neighbors began to say, how is this? There is no one by that name, its unfamiliar to us. They beckoned for Zacharias to respond and he asked for a writing table and wrote, "His name is John," and his mouth was opened, and his tongue was immediately loosed (Luke 1:59-65). Notice how as a Father, he had to cooperate with God concerning the destiny of his son John. This is an outstanding example of how important the roles of Fatherhood and Manhood are in the lives of both our wives and children, and my prayer is that you and I as Men would embrace our great responsibility as Men and engage in our God given *Authority to give proper identity to this generation.*

CHAPTER 9

THE POWER
OF PERSONAL VALUE

PROVERBS 16:4

*"God made everything with a place and PURPOSE;
even the wicked are included-but for judgment."*

He Saw a UFO

In this final chapter I'm going to deal with *Personal Value*. I believe that when it pertains to destiny and the fulfilling of our purpose as Men, there is nothing more important. Understanding your personal value as a Man is essential to accomplishing everything that God has designed you to accomplish and without a clear understanding of it, a Man can live his entire life projecting blame on others as to why he has not fulfilled his dreams and goals in life. Earlier in the book I mentioned that God never creates anything or anyone without purpose. We find in the book of Proverbs chapter 16:4 (MSG) it states, "God made everything with a place and purpose." Also, in the book of Ecclesiastes 3:1 is says, "To everything there is a season, and a time to every *purpose* under heaven." The word purpose means "A reason for existing." There isn't one Man walking this beautiful planet that doesn't have a reason for existing. Sadly, there are many men who don't know what they are here for, and when a Man doesn't know his purpose for living, then that Man can become self-destructive and self-sabotage his own destiny. What's worse is that not only will he become self-destructive and self-sabotaging, he will also project that same thing upon his wife, his children, and every other relationship that he has. This is why I believe that the *Blueprint* is so vitally important to Men today from every walk of life. I believe it is the answer to the pain and dissatisfaction that's in the hearts of many Men. Proverbs 29:18 tells us when a man doesn't have vision, sight, or insight into his reason for existing, he will cast off restraint. That means there is nothing to create boundaries or self-discipline in that man's life. Men without purpose become alcoholics, sex addicts, abusive to their families, and much more. But when a Man finds his purpose, it creates vision, boundaries, and discipline in that man's life, because a Man needs to have a problem to solve, a target to hit, a race to run, a challenge to face and overcome, because that's how God wired us as Men. Years ago, I heard one Man tell a story about a young man who saw a UFO. He had me intrigued while he was telling this humorous story. He said that there was a young Man who never bathed or brushed his teeth or took care of himself. He never dressed well or combed his hair, he just didn't care. Until one day, this young Man saw a UFO. Then he began to tell us that the UFO the young Man saw was an Unidentified Female Object. I laughed so hard because I could see it right in front of my eyes. That UFO he saw gave him Vision; he now had a sense of purpose, so he started bathing, combing his hair, and brushing his teeth because he had something to aim at that he wanted in life. He had something that motivated him to be a better Man. Now all of a sudden he had some discipline and boundaries in his life because he wanted to get that UFO, he wanted that (Unidentified Female Object).

On the Edge of My Seat

When a Man finds his purpose, then he finds his reason for existence, when he discovers his *why*, then like the young Man and the UFO, he will begin to adjust things in his life, he will begin to discipline himself and create safe boundaries to ensure that he gets to his desired destination. When a Man discovers his *why* or his purpose, then his confidence kicks in because he is comfortable with who he is and has discovered his *why* in life. I call this discovering, defining, and determining personal significance. I have learned a lot about the importance of discovering, defining, and determining your personal significance because as I said at the beginning of this book, it's been my personal self-discovery journey in life. When you look the word *Significance* up it just simply means *Importance*, and that is what I believe that Men want; we want to know that we are necessary, we want to know that we are important. Every Man has been wired with *Significance* that will solve specific problems that only he is able to solve. I believe that our greatest dilemma in life is that most haven't discovered their significance, thus leaving them unfulfilled in life. One day I was at a conference at my Pastor's Church and I was on the edge of my seat as he was teaching the word, and my spirit was burning with great hunger for my personal significance. I was desperate for his voice and direction pertaining to my destiny. There were thousands in the room, but I felt as if it was only my heavenly Father and me. I began to inquire of the lord pertaining to my *why*, and in that moment, The Holy Spirit spoke to me something that would change me forever, He said, "Significance is when you become so necessary that the world cannot function properly without your impact." Right there I saw exactly what He was teaching me. He was letting me know that my significance would determine my value and my value would then be undeniable, because there is no one else anywhere like *ME*! So, then I understood that for me to become the real *ME* was my greatest priority, second to my intimate relationship with Jesus, because my *why*, my *Significance* was key to fulfilling my *Purpose* in life. It was that which made ME Valuable.

From Volunteer to Valuable

I heard a story about a Man by the name of Bud Everhart. He always had a desire to work in aviation. He started off volunteering at an aircraft mechanic shop and just did whatever was necessary. Bud learned just about everything he could about the trade while simply volunteering. It was time for him to take some time off, so he treated it like it was a real job and went to the boss and told him he would be off, and the boss responded by saying "Bud, no problem, you don't work here so go ahead take the time off." Bud took the time off but something spectacular happened while he was off. The boss began to see that certain things that he needed done weren't getting completed. Then the boss went around the shop and began asking why they weren't getting done and the other mechanics said, "That's Bud's job." Then the boss said, "Let's get Bud back in here." Bud became significant; his value was enlarged to the degree that they could not function properly without him. He learned every job and completed tasks that no one else could do and that made him valuable, so valuable that they had to hire him. This is a great example for any young Man.

Often I talk to young Men and they are in College and they generally don't really know what they want out of life. I then tell them to get busy with another Man's vision. Value what's valuable to another Man and God in turn will increase your personal value. I also tell young Men *Don't work for money, work for purpose.* There are two reasons why I always say that, one being that if you work for money then money will always control your decision making. A Man must not be controlled by money; Jesus teaches us that in Matthew 6:24 that you cannot serve both God and mammon. Mammon is the currency by which this fallen world system operates and many men have forfeited their destiny because they never prioritized their self-development to discover their personal significance and value. The late Dr. Myles Munroe said years ago that the graveyard was the richest place in the world because therein lies potential, significance, and purpose that was never actualized and fulfilled. The second reason I tell young

Men not to work for money is because "No Man has the capacity to pay you what you're truly worth." When we work for others, we are to view that as a part of our assignment. We are to glean knowledge, wisdom, and skill from those experiences that would help us develop our significance, and thus increase our personal value. Again, Proverbs 23:7 says that you are the direct reflection of what you THINK about you! Not what others think about you! The word *Thinketh* here in Proverbs means to *Estimate or determine the value of.* You must think the right thoughts about yourself, you determine your own *value*, and you determine your own worth. This is so *powerful* because this literally removes all excuses from a Man's life as to why he is successful or not. As a Man, you and I have been wired in such a way that no man has *power* to cause you to fail except yourself. A man's boundaries are not outside of him, they are not the people or the circumstances that he is around or experiencing. His boundaries are a product of his own self perception of himself. Again, please remember that *Our perception of people, places, and things is always a projection of ourselves.* You and I as Men *see* everything through the lens of our Self-Image. I often say that I thank God for everything that people haven't done for me because sometimes what others do for you cripple your personal development. So many people continue to lean on the arm of others rather than leaning on God. The more dependent that I am on God as Father, the less dependent I am on any Man! Every Man discovers himself through his dependency upon God as father and this is extremely important because the world is looking for those who are *Significant*, and its significant individuals that solve the problems of hurting humanity.

"It was entirely different"

One day years ago I was recording at a studio in the Metro Detroit area. I was working on my first solo album and had a certain song mixed at this particular studio. When I finished I asked the engineer what he thought about the song. The reason I asked him was because He engineered for some well-known artists from my area; all these artists were secular artists and I was a Christian Rap artist, and I wanted to get his opinion on the song because I knew its content was different than everything else he has ever done. After I asked the question he told me that it sounded great, even though it was Christian rap and it was different. Then he began to say, "Nothing surprises me as far as music now days," I then said why? He responded by telling me that some years back he was recording a group from our area called D12 and a young skinny white rapper came in with them. He was quiet and had a hoodie on and looked somewhat isolated. He then said when the white kid started rapping he sounded like he was talking in the microphone and not rapping. It was entirely different than anything that he ever heard before. He told me, "This kid cannot rap," and the reason he said that about him was because he was different! After telling me that story, he divulged to me that the artist was Eminem. I was blown away. That story never left me because to me it paints the great value of being *Significant*. We all know what happened after that, Eminem changed the entire way Rap was being done. His significance made him stand out, but in order for him to stand out and be distinct, he first had to lose sight of what others thought about him and how he rapped. He had to be willing to be bold and stand up! Not one of us as Men has been created without personal significance. There is something about you as a Man that should make you stand out in the crowd! But like the example I just gave, you must be willing to be different and stand up!

What do I mean about this statement stand up and stand out? I'm glad you asked. Most don't stand up for *who* they are because *who* you are is completely different than everyone around you. That's why one of the greatest difficulties you will ever experience is *being* yourself. Why? The reason is because everyone loves you when you are like them. People only have difficulty with you when you are different, and the reason is that your personal significance causes others to see their own personal limitations, and when I am saying personal limitations, I am meaning the limitations that they have placed upon themselves. When you discover your significance, it gives others permission to become who God created them to BE.

It's Hard Not BEING You

The book of Proverbs says in chapter 13:15 "Good understanding gives favor: But the Way of the TRANSGRESSOR is hard." I interpreted this verse completely wrong for years. I was so sin conscious that I only, shallowly, viewed it as a verse that was talking about someone who is living in sin will experience difficulty and hardship throughout their lives. But after carefully picking this verse apart one day, the Holy Spirit helped me gain true insight into what it actually means. The word *transgressor* here means one who covers, or one who acts covertly. It's speaking of an individual who deals deceitfully. To act covertly is to cover up and hide the truth. Wow, for the first time I saw it. This individual was *being* someone that he was not! A Transgressor hides the *truth* of who he is and acts or pretends to be someone that he is not. The next thing is that the word *way* here is speaking of a course or a road. When you put these two words and their true meaning together, it's saying that the Man who covers or hides his real self, his significance, his value; his way or course or life will be hard. It literally means that it's very hard being who you were not created to BE. Think of this. When Michael Jackson was alive, it would be hard for him to be a professional basketball player, why? Because he was created to sing. How about Michael Jordan, it would be hard for him to sing the *Star Spangled Banner*, Why? Because he was created to be one of the greatest athletes to ever live. It's hard for any Man to BE anything other than *who* God has created him to BE!

"It's hard being you"

It's also hard to BE who God created you to BE because as I said, People are afraid when others discover their significance, because it causes them to have to face themselves and their own personal fears of standing up and standing out. This understanding has caused me to discover something extremely important and that is this; Significance will attract to you those who belong in your sphere of influence, but significance will also repel from you those who do not belong in your sphere of influence. There are those who will celebrate you because they too have discovered their significance. Only significant individuals can celebrate the success of others. Then there are those that will just tolerate you because their lack of significance won't allow them to be happy for you. Not everyone can *Go with you* because not everyone will be willing to *Grow with you*. There are those in your life that as you grow in your personal significance and value, you will outgrow those relationships. If you are going to achieve your destiny and stand out and be significant, then as a Man you're going to have to grow some tough skin because not everyone is going to like you when you become you! Jesus had those who loved him, but not everyone loved him, some hated him. Always remember that significance will attract favor as well as frustration to your life.

There's Enough to Pass Around

I have also discovered that people who don't know who they are, are often critical towards those who have discovered, defined, and are determining their significance and personal value. This truly is done out of fear! The fear of lack and limitation causes individuals to respond in such a manner. The truth is that as I said before, *God never creates anything or anyone without purpose.* There is enough purpose to pass around, Halleluiah! It's a scarcity mentality that plagues individuals with a mindset of limitation, shortage, and lack. We need to understand as Men that if the Lord is our Shepherd, we shall not lack or be deficient in any area of our lives. God is no respecter of persons, but he is a respecter of faith. You and I as Men don't get from God what we deserve, we get what we believe and if a Man's belief system is altered, he constantly thinks that God has given someone something that he hasn't given him, then that person will waste all their creative capacity on complaining and criticism rather than discovering, defining, and determining his own significance and personal value. I learned this personally and I would like to share it with you. I was probably the very first Gospel rapper who received a national distribution deal in the state of Michigan. I was signed to the largest independent one stop Christian distribution company in the USA. They created a subsidiary company that specialized in my genre of music, and I released approximately 12 full albums worldwide through my independent record label. During those years there were a lot of up and coming artists just like myself, and we all networked and worked together for the advancement of the kingdom of God. Every one of us were probably experiencing just about the same level of success in the industry, and no one at that time was standing out more than the others.

No Competition

I remember clearly in 2005, I was sitting with the staff of this particular company and I thank God for these individuals because they were tremendous in their skill to promote and sell Christian rap music. We were all there in an office and another record label sent in some T Shirts and music as part of their submission to the company seeking independent distribution. The main artist owned his own label and was well known but was seeking distribution for his artists that were signed to his label. One of the reps from the distribution company held up their T Shirt and said, "what do you think Big Shadow?" (Big Shadow was my rap name) I said, "we are all on the same team." Little did I know, this artist and his label would become the largest artist and Christian record label ever to surface in our genre of music. As he began to rise to prominence and as the Lord began to give him more influence, myself and many other artists began to become critical and started complaining about why we thought he was succeeding, and why we weren't reaching the platform that he had attained. My favorite excuse for myself was "He compromised to get there, and I have standards." Then one day the Lord began to speak to me and deal with my heart. He said to me, "Claude, the reason why you are bothered with this is due to your own lack of significance and personal value." I had to humble myself, repent, and change my thinking. Since then I stopped being critical of my brother in Christ and his success; I now celebrate him. Even if I don't necessarily agree with everything he may be doing, I still celebrate him. Why? It's simple; I have discovered my significance and personal value. As Men, we must learn that in God's Kingdom, there is no competition! We are all unique and we all have purpose. Here's a simple example; If I sit down at my table and eat a full course meal and I am full and satisfied, then when I come to your house I don't have to reach into your refrigerator for food because I am not hungry. What does this mean? A Man that has discovered his "significance and personal value" wont waste creative time criticizing another Man for his success because he is already *Fully satisfied*, he is too focused on his potential and purpose to be critical about another Man's. Decide right now, like I did, to repent and change your thinking about being critical and complaining about any individual. You and I are Men, Men aren't critical complainers, Men create, and you can't create and be critical complainers simultaneously.

The Significant Son

Matthew 8:23-27, "And when he was entered into a ship, his disciples followed him. And, behold, there arose a great tempest in the sea, insomuch that the ship was covered with the waves: but he was asleep. And his disciples came to him, saying, Lord, save us: we perish. And he saith unto them, why are ye fearful, O ye of little faith? Then he arose and rebuked the winds and the sea; and there was a great calm. But

the MEN marveled, saying, what manner (Kind) of MAN is this, that
even the winds and the sea obey him!

Jesus was a great example of what it means to be significant and valuable. He was distinct, he wasn't like any other, and He was in a class all by himself. When I read about Jesus, it amazes me every time because he stood out in the crowd regardless of environment, culture, conditions, or circumstances. Jesus remained his true self and to me that's what made him so valuable. When you read Matthew 8:23-27, there is a fascinating story about Jesus as he calms what one translation calls a "Violent storm." This storm was so furious that it was overwhelming to the disciples who were seasoned fishermen. Another account of this story say's that Jesus was calmly asleep on a pillow in the ship as the raging waves, influenced by the winds, beat upon both the exterior and interior of their ship. This was not a small storm; this storm had to be a very large one due to the Greek word used for *Tempest* here. The word used is the word *Seismos*, which is where we get our word *Seismic* when we are describing a seismic event. An earthquake is something that we use the word *Seismic* for so that should give you a picture of what kind of storm this was. Also, this boat was not a canoe, it was a ship and the scripture say's that the ship was covered by the waves. I think it's necessary for us to see how serious this event was, in order that we may extract the importance of Jesus role during this adverse circumstance. Regardless of this antagonistic environment, His significance stood out like an apple in a bushel of oranges, he was different than every man there. It's important that we know that he was experiencing the same problems that they were experiencing. They were afraid, fearful, overcome, and thinking that this could be the last day of their lives because they thought they would drown. They were hopeless! At least that's what they thought. Then Jesus, out of his significance, the most valuable Man on the ship, spoke to the wind and commanded the sea to be calm and there was a great peace that came upon everything and every man present. Notice the response the disciples made in Verse 27, it says that "The Men were amazed and asked, 'What kind of Man is this? Even the winds and the waves obey him!'" This is a powerful story because it's just one of the many that depict the significance of Jesus. His significance and personal value empowered him to be a problem solver during an impossible circumstance.

The Conclusion: Confession

I personally believe that God is raising up a group of Men that are going to solve the problems of hurting humanity just like Jesus did. I believe that there is a generation of Men that are dissatisfied with the low level, limited way of thinking that has plagued humanity. I believe that these Men are those who have seen the destruction and the breakdown in marriage and family and how it has shaped community. I believe that these Men are ready to take full responsibility and resist the current status quo of society and cultural decadence. I believe that we are these Men! And we are those who are intimately acquainted with the Father (Intimacy), those who know who we are in Christ (Identity), and we are those who have discovered, defined, and are determining our personal significance and have become so valuable that the world can't function properly without our impact (Destiny). We have come to an end of the understanding of Manhood that has evolved out of this fallen world system and have embraced *The Blueprint*. We are those who are taking responsibility for the problems that this generation is facing. We are those who have come to an end of selfishness and are selflessly walking in love. We are those who are accountable one to another and interdependently connecting and resourcing one another's lives. We are those who are healing marriages, families, churches, communities, neighborhoods, cities, and nations everywhere! We are those who stand up and boldly stand out in the midst of darkness. We are the light of the world and we are the salt of the earth! And when people are bound afflicted, tormented, wounded, broken, divorced, suicidal, and without hope and completely overcome by the storms of life, we are the Men that will speak to the wind and command the waves to be calm and they will say of you and I, *"What kind of MAN is This."* **"Change the Men, Change the World"**

THE TURN CHALLENGE

The "Turn Challenge" is a nine-month Discipleship program created for the development of Men of all ages, ethnicities and all backgrounds. This curriculum is built on three-principles; (Intimacy, Identity and Destiny.) These principles construct each Man from the inside out equipping them with the ability to, "Know God, know themselves and know their purpose in life." Some of the key components learned are Accountability, Servant leadership, Principles for developing intimacy with God, Faithfulness and much more. For more information please visit our website.

www.claudebevier.org

"Bridging the Gap Between Generations."

The "Restore World Tour" is a movement born out of Malachi 4:6 Restoring the hearts of the Fathers back to the children, and the hearts of the children back to their fathers and giving this generation its proper identity. This Tour stands out among the crowd by gathering the entire family together with an aim to "Bridge the gap between Generations." The Restore Tour utilizes various forms of metdia such as music, literature, drama, and film to bring awareness to the #1 epidemic of Fatherlessness. For more information or to BOOK the "Restore World Tour" for you next event, please visit our website.

www.restoreworldtour.com

About the Author

 Claude E. Bevier is a husband, father, grandfather and spiritual father to many. He and His lovely wife Rosa are the founders and Pastors of Restore World Church of Adrian and Romulus, Michigan. Their very humble beginnings began in a 3-bedroom apartment with 14 people which were mainly children and teenagers. Since the inception of their ministry, they have ministered to hundreds of people and have become "Dad and Mom" to an entire community. Claude is an entrepreneur, business owner, life coach and motivational speaker with a passion to "Bridge the gap between Generations"

Claude was trained and served as youth Pastor under the leadership of Pastor's Henry and Connie Healey of Christian Life Center Church of Ypsilanti, Michigan, during which time he traveled extensively as an evangelist, ministering in prisons, high schools and juvenile detention centers. During these travels he ministered through the avenue of gospel rap music under the gospel rap name of B.I.G Shadow, which means Believing in God's Image.

In 2012 Claude submitted to the leadership of Dr.'s Bill and Veronica Winston, Pastors of Living Word Christian Center Church and is ordained as a pastor of the Faith Ministers Alliance.

In 2016, Claude and his wife Rosa launched The Restore Tour. A movement born out of Malachi 4:6 Restoring the hearts of the Fathers back to the children, and the hearts of the children back to their fathers and giving this generation its proper identity. This Tour utilizes various forms of media such as music, literature, drama, and film to bring awareness to this epidemic of Fatherlessness.

CPSIA information can be obtained
at www.ICGtesting.com
Printed in the USA
FFHW010622231019
55714527-61570FF